Today's Youth, Tomorrow's Leaders

PRAISE FOR *TODAY'S YOUTH, TOMORROW'S LEADERS*

"Smita Guha's book reminds us all that standards alone will not improve the educational and developmental gains of our children. We must leverage student achievement with a focused understanding of how children grow and learn in healthy and nurturing environments that foster personal growth, individual learning, and relationships. In a market saturated with guidance on outcomes based achievement, *Today's Youth, Tomorrow's Leaders* offers a refreshing focus on the substantive process of educating our children. She offers detailed guidance to both families and schools.

In our steadfast desire to raise student achievement, we must remember that the world of tomorrow demands that our children be college and career ready and also prepared with a keen understanding of themselves, their learning, and their relationships with those around them. This book offers a practical approach to practitioner and parent alike in supporting such learning environments and opportunities." —**Eric Contreras**, assistant superintendent, former high school principal, New York City Department of Education

"A good early childhood experience contributes immeasurably to helping children become responsible adults who care about and show concern for others. In this practical and inspirational guide, Guha explains the major theories and developmental topics on which sound early childhood principles and practices are based. This book contains clear and concise research findings and examples of sensitive and supportive advice for those who teach and care for children." —**Cathleen S. Soundy**, professor of early childhood education, Temple University

"In this timely addition to recent work on the teaching and learning of children, Guha reminds us that for all children to grow into empathetic, creative, responsible, life-long learners, we adults—as teachers, parents, and community—must lead the way. She helps us, throughout this thoughtful book, with real strategies and ideas, to nurture our youth to become tomorrow's leaders! —**Brett Elizabeth Blake**, professor at St. John's University in Queens; coauthor of *Teaching All Children to Read*

"Guha offers significant insight into the key elements that, when combined, can greatly influence the future trajectory for young people. It is a solid and foundational text that can be a beneficial resource for classroom educators and administrators alike." —**Randolph A. Ford**, principal, The Abigail Adams School, New York

Today's Youth, Tomorrow's Leaders

How Parents and Educators Can Influence and Guide the Learning Process

Dr. Smita Guha

ROWMAN & LITTLEFIELD EDUCATION

A division of
ROWMAN & LITTLEFIELD
Lanham • Boulder • New York • Toronto • Plymouth, UK

Published by Rowman & Littlefield Education
A division of Rowman & Littlefield
4501 Forbes Boulevard, Suite 200, Lanham, Maryland 20706
www.rowman.com

10 Thornbury Road, Plymouth PL6 7PP, United Kingdom

British Library Cataloguing in Publication Information Available

Library of Congress Cataloging-in-Publication Data

Guha, Smita, 1965–
Today's youth, tomorrow's leaders : how parents and educators can influence and guide the learning process / Smita Guha.
     pages cm
Includes bibliographical references.
ISBN 978-1-4758-0248-1 (cloth : alk. paper) — ISBN 978-1-4758-0250-4 (electronic) 1. Child rearing. 2. Child development. I. Title.
  HQ769.G925 2013
  305.231—dc23   2013036104

∞™ The paper used in this publication meets the minimum requirements of American National Standard for Information Sciences—Permanence of Paper for Printed Library Materials, ANSI/NISO Z39.48-1992.

Printed in the United States of America

DEDICATION

This book is affectionately dedicated to my two daughters,
Amrita Guha and Anandita Guha.

Contents

Acknowledgments

Thanks to:

My husband, Mr. Amit Guha, for his help with the title of the book.

My sister, Ms. Snigdha Dutta, and brother, Mr. Samaresh Bose, for their inspiration.

My colleagues Dr. Brett Elizabeth Blake, Dr. Mary Beth Schaefer, and Dr. Joanne M. Robertson-Eletto for reviewing the book and offering helpful suggestions.

The editor Mr. Tom Koerner for his recommendations and encouraging remarks.

Introduction

This book consists of seven chapters and each chapter is designed to present ideas and research on ways to help make children successful in life. However, each chapter is a stand-alone entity, and is non-sequential. Readers can choose to read any chapter to gain specific insights in helping children.

Chapter 1 talks about how important it is to introduce children to exploring. Children not only learn from the adults but also learn from exploring the environment. The environment is the third teacher. It is important for adults to provide children with a rich environment where children can touch and feel things with no fear. A print-rich environment exposes children to the whole word; it helps children to develop reading readiness skills, such as identifying letters and relating texts to real life. Children are naturally drawn to environmental print. Adults can help children to decode words if needed.

The rationale behind chapter 2 is no matter what, children will grow up, but it is the adult who has a big responsibility to help children grow up to be good citizens. It is very important for adults to learn the basics of child development. Every child has unique capabilities but each also shares common characteristics with his or her age group and culture group.

Chapter 3 advocates for the importance of home, school, and community partnerships. With the home, school, and community working together, all can help in the development of the children. It is true that home and school are part of the community, but in this book community refers to outside of home and school. It refers to how parents, teachers, and school administrators can all work together to bring rich experiences for all children.

In order to learn how and why children behave in a certain way, it is of utmost importance to keep a record of children's behavior. Chapter 4 talks not only about the importance of observation and documentation but also shows the readers how to observe, when to observe, and what to observe. This chapter also shows different ways of documentation with examples to get a whole picture of each individual child and also a child with other children and adults.

Teachers generally spend a lot of time developing curriculum for the children. Chapter 5 notes the need for teachers to go beyond the four walls of the classroom. Curriculum could be evolving according to the interests of the children. It is with that interest from the children that teachers could teach various subject areas. Further, parents should also seek those interests in their children and offer help, or they could also seek help from the teachers.

Nutrition education in chapter 6 plays a vital role in children's development. Children should be fed nutritious food from the very start and also should be made aware of healthy and unhealthy food. Children in their surrounding environment are exposed to food through various media; it is the significant adult who will teach about healthy eating habits and make a difference in the lives of children. Further, the safety of children is of utmost importance to all adults involved.

The last chapter summarizes all the important ideas throughout the book. The salient ideas in the book move toward a single goal: to help children to grow and develop in a nurturing environment. Children are valued members of society. It is the children of today who will make better lives for everyone tomorrow.

Chapter One

Introducing Children to a Kind, Caring, and Just World

The leader's able stewardship makes the world a better place. It is the child of today who will become the efficient leader of tomorrow, making decisions for us all. It is certainly true that "it takes a village to raise a child," but the role of the caretaker cannot be underestimated. A child needs to be loved and cared for, taught how to become a good human being, and then he or she will reciprocate these understandings to others; thus, the seeds of good deeds are spread.

As we all work together to facilitate children in their developmental process, and instill values in them, we benefit by creating a conducive living environment of our own. Our nurtured children will become the future world policymakers, taking bold steps toward rightful decisions. Some will become scientists creating great inventions, and some will be explorers finding exciting discoveries, and in all they will be making history.

As we parents and teachers guide children through the developmental process, the most important quality that one must possess is patience. As a patient listener, we hear children's tender voices, lend our shoulders for their cries, sympathize in their sorrows, and rejoice in their achievements.

In order to meet their needs, we must understand them first. We must always look for clues. Their body language, their oral narratives, their expressions through art or through music tell us so much. Only if we understand them well can we take the appropriate supportive action to help them grow. For example, an infant communicates his or her needs by crying; the infant could be hungry, sleepy, or having pain or any physical discomfort that urges him or her to cry. Addressing those issues at that moment provides a great deal of comfort, and gives the child warmth and a sense of security he or she needs. If the infant during that time does not get what he or she needs, then the child feels the world to be a cold and cruel place.

Adults must realize that children need to think of the world as a warm and welcoming world. A positive outlook is important. Their behavioral stance influences their actions. So, it is better to emphasize the positive rather than the negative. For example, it is better if adults explain to a child how he or she is expected to behave rather than uttering "no" all the time. Theorists believe that when children hear "no," they get confused and do not know how to behave or even react. For example, if adults want children to walk and "not run," then it is better to say "walk" than to say "don't run." They need to be specific in their direction.

Adults must be good role models. According to theorist Jean Piaget (1954), children like to imitate adults. Therefore, adults' behavior influences the way that children behave. All children like to be praised. Behaviorists believe that it is better to praise the children for their good behavior and ignore the negative. Of course, if the child's safety is of concern, then the adult must interfere.

Young children are so valuable and yet so vulnerable that we have a lifelong mission and obligation to educate, inspire, and develop the best possible leaders for tomorrow. We not only wish to educate them but also to protect them, guide them, and offer them a future with hope and promise. We want to provide them with a platform upon which to develop to their fullest potential.

Every child is unique and childhood is a valuable time in one's life. Children should be active learners and be engaged in meaningful learning experiences. According to the constructivists' learning theory, children construct meaning from their experiences; however, adults need to create those active learning opportunities for them.

This book provides readers with a number of guiding tools for adults to assist children in all areas of development, and help them to grow physically, cognitively, socially, and emotionally. To become a good human being is the first and most important step.

SUMMARY

- It is the adults' responsibility to nurture children in becoming successful in the future as citizens of society.
- Our nurtured children will become the future world leaders making policies, and take the bold steps in rightful decisions. Some will be scientists making great inventions, and some will be explorers making new discoveries, and in all they will be creating history.
- An important quality to have when working with children is to be a patient listener who understands children's body language, oral narratives, and expressions. Adults should look for clues on how to assist them.
- Adults must be good role models and provide a positive outlook to children.
- Creative, active, learning environments provide opportunities for children to grow and become successful leaders of tomorrow.

Thinking Questions

1. How can you help children to think that they have come to a kind, caring, and just world?
2. List all the caring attributes necessary to ensure children's trust in this world.

REFERENCE

Piaget, J. (1954). *The construction of reality in the child.* New York: Basic Books.

Chapter Two

Helping Young Children Grow and Learn

BASICS OF CHILD DEVELOPMENT

For decades, child development has been a major research focus of educational psychology. Theorists and researchers alike have observed and studied child behavior and offered their suggestions. Their thoughts converge in some ways, but differ in others. For example, Piaget (1954) states that children go through stages of development, with every stage possessing a certain distinguishing feature. Children need to be actively involved through direct experiences with the physical world. The basic premise of Piaget's cognitive theory is that intelligence develops over time. Intelligence is referred to as the cognitive or mental process by which children acquire knowledge. Piaget also identified two stages of moral thinking: "heteronomy," being governed by others regarding right or wrong; and "autonomy," being governed by oneself regarding right or wrong.

It is during the early childhood years that adults need to help children grow up as responsible citizens. In each stage children need to be well stimulated. Children learn actively by doing, and their capacity to learn depends on a combination of genetics and environmental conditions. Gesell (1949) believes that all learning is determined by biological readiness.

The behaviorists, on the other hand, emphasized that all behavior has a cause and that all behavior results from reinforcement received from the environment. According to Thorndike's Law of Effect, if a satisfying incident follows a behavior, the individual tends to repeat the behavior. Skinner emphasized the role of the environment in providing people with clues that reinforce their behavior. To summarize the above, behaviorists state all behavior is learned, and all behavior is caused by reinforcers from which individuals gain pleasure of some kind. All children enjoy receiving attention. According to behaviorists, when a child receives attention, that attention works to reinforce behavior. Praise, for example, is a reinforcer.

Adults have to empower children and help them learn that they are primarily responsible for their own behavior. It is important to offer children choices and give them responsibilities. Vygotsky (1930), a prominent Russian child development theorist, mentioned that social interactions provide children opportunities for learning from each other so that they obtain higher levels of thinking and behavior. Vygotsky called this "scaffolding." Scaffolding is an important social interaction that takes places between children. It is a skill that children learn from a very early age.

According to the National Association for the Education of Young Children (NAEYC), children can be grouped as follows:

Infants:	birth to one or two years
Toddlers:	one or two years to three years
Preschoolers:	three years to five years
Kindergarteners:	five years to six years
Primary:	six years to eight years

From the above groups and through consideration of the basics of child development, educators have categorized four different domains of development: they are physical, social, cognitive, and emotional. Other forms of development, such as psychosocial and creative, fall under these categories. Physical development can be further divided into two categories: gross motor and fine motor development.

In analyzing the importance of physical development, both educators and health professionals posit that an hour of daily physical exercise is mandatory for children. They stress the importance of cultivating good nutritional habits at an early age, which is quite important given the prevalence of headlines in newspapers today about childhood obesity and overweight children. This concern is shared by schools and communities, which by and large emphasize the importance of balanced diets that include fruits and vegetables. In addition to physical education, an important aspect of gross motor exercise, fine motor exercise is also crucial. While technology and computers lead the way in forms of communication, the very basics of holding a pencil to write should be addressed in a child's early years, because such exercises demonstrate one's fine motor skills. Likewise, engaging in exercises such as the pincer grasp (using forefinger and thumb), lacing, tracing, cutting with scissors, gluing, and coloring are effective ways to enhance children's fine motor skills.

The next form of child development is cognitive. Researchers believe that children need to be read to even before they are born. It is suggested that even when the baby is in the mother's womb, parents should turn on gentle music and let the baby hear the sounds of their voices.

Studies show that music—and more specifically, musical patterns—influences children's understanding of mathematical concepts. Experts find a high correlation between musical talent and mathematical skills in children; however, it should be noted that the inverse is not supported. It is believed that parents are the first teachers of their children, followed by their classroom teachers, and then the environment around them. As educators and proponents of childhood education, we feel that the more children are stimulated by meaningful learning experiences, the better they develop cognitively.

Once the seeds for positive cognitive development are sown in a child's early years, they are more likely to yield positive developmental outcomes in the long term. Every child needs emotional care, intellectual stimulation, an enriched learning environment, and parents and teachers who facilitate each one of these aspects.

It is during the early childhood years that children learn how to get along with others. Adults need to demonstrate how a child should interact with others and treat others exactly the way he or she wants to be treated. This has been thoroughly supported by Maria Montessori, who stated that adults must treat every child with respect. Only then will children will be able to show respect to others.

As children grow, their social surroundings become more meaningful to them. Vygotsky (1930) posits that this is true because children learn within social groups, and their transitions to social human beings occur within these spaces; thus, adults are charged with the responsibility of helping children be successful socially by creating opportunities for them to intermingle with peers, older children, or even with adults. To live in harmony with society, children need to learn how to behave and interact with one another.

Adults can provide social guidance in a number of key ways. They must convey norms and customs to children, teach them how to be kind and gentle, and identify the boundaries of inappropriate and appropriate societal behaviors for them. During social interactions between children, it is often seen that children behave in ways that are not acceptable to adults—for example, grabbing a toy, biting, or pushing another child. We all make mistakes in social settings, but it is important for adults to let children know why they've erred, rather than simply requiring the perfunctory "sorry." It is the reflection that will help the child.

We must remember that children who are happy are better able to develop emotionally. A child who has peace of mind also has the ability to stay focused. That child, in turn, becomes a better learner. We want to see children happy most of the time; if a child is unhappy for most of the time, adults need to take care of the child immediately. An unhappy child is deprived or neglected. It is incumbent upon the adults in the children's life to assist them in their transitions from feeling sad or really sorry to being in full pursuit of happiness.

In order to assist children to become better learners, educators have created *Developmentally Appropriate Practice* (Copple & Bredekamp, 2009). *Developmentally Appropriate Practice* has three dimensions: age appropriateness, individual appropriateness, and cultural appropriateness. Although children do exhibit some characteristics according to their age, they also exhibit certain individual characteristics due to cultural experiences; children can behave differently, even though they might be the same age.

Erikson (1950) describes lifelong development in eight universal stages. The first four stages address the early years; the remaining four cover the years from adolescence to adulthood.

- Trust vs. Mistrust (0–12 months). Children at this age need to develop a sense of trust toward parents, teachers, and caregivers.
- Autonomy vs. Shame and Doubt (1–3 years). Children need to gain control over certain behaviors such as eating, sleeping, and going to the bathroom. If children are not given that opportunity, they may doubt their capabilities later in life.
- Initiative vs. Guilt (3–5 years). During this stage, children need to gain control over their everyday lives using social interaction.

- Identity vs. Confusion (12–20 years). Children need to learn about themselves and their heritage through their relationships with others.
- Intimacy vs. Isolation (early adulthood). Young adults explore and form intimate relationships.
- Generativity vs. Stagnation (middle adulthood). During this stage, individuals focus on their families and careers, and develop ways to contribute to society.
- Integrity vs. Despair (old age). During this stage, individuals reflect on their lives and form a sense of satisfaction or dissatisfaction.

Since the first four stages deal with children, this book will mainly highlight the roles adults play in children's lives during those times. It is important to note that such roles can be positive or negative; the kinds of signals adults send children about appropriate and inappropriate behaviors will impact them far beyond these early years, and influence their developing worldviews.

It is important for adults to emphasize the positive and avoid the negative. It is important for adults to mention what is expected from a child rather than what is not wanted. For example, if you want the child to talk and not shout, then state "please talk." It is not advisable to say "don't shout." Children get confused about their expected behavior. Further, children do not like to be told "no." Therefore, it is better, if at all possible, to avoid the negative when speaking with young children. Moreover, adults are role models and children try to imitate adult behavior. Therefore, it is important for adults to demonstrate appropriate behavior "to talk" and "not to shout."

Adults should be consistent and fair in their behavior toward children. Thus, rationalizing and explaining why certain things are inappropriate, rather than just saying "because I said so," ultimately helps children. It is also necessary for adults to treat children with respect. Children know that adults have more power and are authority figures in their lives, and are more likely to respect adults if they receive respect in turn. This was a central tenet of Montessori's teachings; she believed all children deserve and expect respect from the adults in their lives.

Adults also play an important role in influencing children's self-esteem. All children have strengths and weaknesses; adults should highlight children's strengths and work to help bolster areas of weakness. For example, if a child is weak in math and strong in language, teachers should point out how much of language is in math, especially in word problems. Teachers could even partner children who are relatively strong in language with those strong in math and encourage them to learn from each other, so that both benefit. Children should never feel as if they are failures in certain areas, because thinking this way quickly leads them to "give up" on subjects. Thus, parents, guardians, caregivers, and teachers, all of whom play pivotal roles in influencing a child's perception of his or her own skills, need to be extremely careful about their use of words. In the end, a child who has self-esteem is more likely to become a successful adult.

It is also important to redirect children's attention in positive ways. If adults help children, the children can help others. Adults who show empathy to others teach children empathy. In the same way, if a child is having behavioral issues, adults can play to the egocentricity of the child by requesting he or she help another; in this way, adults correct inappropriate behavior in positive ways. Skinner and Watson argue that development for the most part involves a series of learned behaviors based on an individual's positive and negative interactions with his or her environment (Skinner, 1938). Therefore, it can be said that if they have positive experiences, children will also exhibit positive behaviors.

Sometimes, adults get angry and confused when children exhibit socially inappropriate behaviors; however, it is important, again, to deal with such behaviors in positive, rather than negative, ways. For example, if a child hits another child, an adult may give him a drum to hit, explaining that it is appropriate to hit things like drums when one is upset, but it is always inappropriate to hit another person. A child who is biting another may be given a cracker to eat instead. While giving the child appropriate substitutes, the teacher or caregiver should explain appropriate and inappropriate behavior to the misbehaving child.

Adults also need to be careful about assigning "timeouts" or enforcing other disciplinary actions. The concept of "timeout" started in order to give children opportunities to calm down and reflect on wrongful behaviors. *Discipline* comes from the Latin word *disciplina*, meaning "to teach"—in other words, to "teach self-control." Adults should proactively teach children ways of dealing with anger in order to give them the tools to gain this kind of self-control. For example, squishing a soft ball or meditating for a while can help children release anger. Others purge negative feelings by drawing or painting. With the help of adults, children can develop beneficial avenues to dispel and deal with negative feelings.

Adults insist on asking children to say "please," "thank you," and "sorry." Although these are socially important words, it is important to note that children learn to use them by imitating adults. Thus, adults should act as role models for children, because, according to Piaget, children learn from and mimic such behavior from adults.

However, children do not blindly imitate adults. They associate words in contexts and specific situations. Different situations yield different needs among children. A child has various needs that must be fulfilled: physical, psychological, and learning. Here, it is important to note Maslow's Hierarchy of Needs (1943). In the first tier, Maslow lists physical needs for food, shelter, clothing, rest, proper health, and hygiene, which he believes are basic needs. In the second tier—psychological—he includes security, trust, acceptance, and affection. Finally, access to developmentally appropriate play materials, social experiences, and exposure to literacy-rich environments are all included in the third tier—learning needs. In addition to these, a child also requires respect and self-esteem.

To meet the needs of the children, it is important to develop a team of teachers, parents, and caregivers to share their knowledge about children. Parents and guardians know how children behave at home, whereas teachers know how they behave at school. An effective partnership between the two ultimately benefits the child. Teachers should plan curricula keeping in mind the needs of every child. Likewise, parents should plan appropriate experiences for their children.

It is clear that children learn from their experiences; thus, parents and educators should have the resources to guide them. One such way is to plan field trips, either through school groups led by teachers, or through individual trips arranged by parents as opportunities for family bonding. These trips should strive to incorporate aspects of the community, because children learn what their community has to offer; the experience also reinforces their connection and sense of belonging to communities.

During such experiences and interactions, adults learn from children and children learn from adults. Adults should communicate with children in order to better understand them. Such learning is facilitated by cues from children. Very young children have not yet developed language, but send their own kinds of signals to the adults around them. It is critical to observe children in action and reflect on cues to gauge their emotions. It is important to create an active, engaging, and stimulating environment for all children.

WHAT RESEARCH SAYS ABOUT BRAIN DEVELOPMENT AMONG YOUNG CHILDREN

Educators have long researched brain development among children.

By understanding how the brain learns, educators are able to determine at what developmental level the child is physically, mentally, socially, and cognitively. With more than 100 billion neurons that would stretch more than 60,000 miles, a newborn baby's brain is quite phenomenal! These neurons must generally form connections within the first eight months of a baby's life to foster optimal brain growth and lifelong learning. Mommies, daddies, and caregivers are extremely vital to ensuring babies reach their full potential (Engel-Smothers & Heim, 2009).

"The more knowledge an educator has and applies, the better the children will learn, and our future leaders will be better educated" (Wasserman, 2007). Thus, it is important for parents and educators to gain access to resources that will help them understand all aspects of their child's development.

Brain Development among Babies

A baby's brain develops at a much faster pace than an adult's because, unlike the latter, it is constantly trying to set up new connections. The baby's brain makes more connections than it actually needs and, over time, sheds unused connections. Synapses carrying the most important messages become stronger and stay, while the unused ones are cut out. This process increases flexibility, thereby allowing the brain to better adapt to its environment. Through repeated contact with the physical and social world, the brain is constantly altered and the stimulated connections within its synapses are strengthened.

Important Considerations for Parents and Teachers
Working with Babies

Parents and teachers working with babies should engage in everyday activities that encourage mutual interaction. These include engaging in sensory activities, exploring objects, reading books, and singing simple songs.

Brain Development among Growing Children

Every child learns differently. The ways that children learn vary based on their age and stage of development. Up until the age of five, children tend to use the right hemisphere for almost all learning. Children go through a transition between preschool and elementary school, however. Once a child has reached kindergarten, he or she is expected to learn in a different manner. Before age five, children learn through exploration and play; after age five, children are expected to sit still and learn at a desk or table, a transition that is sometimes extremely hard for many children.

It is important to talk briefly about sequential and non-sequential learning among children. "Sequential knowledge is harder for the brain to process. Nonlinear learning in bits and pieces is easier for the brain to process. Each side of the brain processes differently. When the brain is working as a whole, great potential can be achieved" (Slegers, 1997). When planning curricula, teachers must be aware of these basic brain processes.

As Siegler (2000) mentions, "[E]verything a child sees, hears, thinks, and touches transfers into an electrical activity that is stored into the synapses within the brain. Each time the brain is stimulated, the experience rewires the brain. Information is carried to the brain in synapses. Each day thousands of synapses die off. Information that is not important or relevant will die off while other information that is relevant will be stored in the brain." Montessori describes this same process as a "sensitive period" in a child's mind; she posits that teachers should be able to able to identify such periods as what we call today "teachable moments." Teachable moments occur when the child is ready to learn; this readiness extends to reading.

According to Hart and Risley (1999), young children must be read and spoken to even before they enter formal schooling. Hebb (1949) suggests that, as neuronal pathways are used repeatedly, they begin to change physically and form steadily faster networks. Hebb's principle that "neurons that fire together, wire together" is echoed in the theory of automaticity (LaBerge & Samuels, 1974). As these pathways are used with ever-increasing efficiency, a beginning reader becomes more fluent, creating the necessary "think time" to form new connections.

Squire and Kandel (2000) demonstrate the existence of three areas of the brain involved in the early stages for learning a new skill or procedure: the prefrontal cortex, the parietal cortex, and the cerebellum. These three areas allow a learner to pay attention, to execute the correct movements, and to perform sequential steps.

Based on Brain Research There Are Several Factors that Contribute to Learning among Young Children

- Visuals play an important role in learning. Pictures consistently trump text or oral presentations.
- Children can be stimulated by engaging their five senses. These senses include sight, hearing, taste, smell, and touch.
- Fluent reading is positively associated with comprehension and is thought to contribute to the learner's ability to process the meaning of texts because they expend less effort in recognizing and decoding symbols, and in assigning meaning to words (Bell & Perfetti, 1994). In terms of reading and language acquisition, students' neurons fire as they watch teachers perform or think through information, such as reading for meaning. Learning about Gardner's Theory of Multiple Intelligences (1983) is important for every adult who works with children. While children are gifted, the following table applies. The table shows specific characteristics that identify specific gifts and talents among children.

Table 2.1. Identifying Specific Gifts and Talents among Children

Gifts and Talents among Children	Identification	Multiple Intelligences
Vocabulary	• A child uses advanced vocabulary correctly. • A child asks about a new word he or she has heard and then practices that word.	• *Verbal-Linguistic*—well-developed verbal skills and sensitivity to the sounds, meanings, and rhythms of words.
Information	• A child remembers and makes mental connections between past and present experiences. For instance, a child might spontaneously apply a principle learned about mammals during group time to another lesson, weeks later, concerned with dinosaurs. • When a child masters a new skill, new concept, song, or rhyme with unusual speed. • A child identifies left or right, both in relation to his or her own body and the body of another person, or if he or she understands how to move to the left or right. • Notice when a child is able to carry out complex instructions to do several things in succession or when a boy or girl is able to absorb several new concepts in a single session.	• *Naturalist*—ability to recognize and categorize plants, animals, and other objects in nature. • *Musical*—ability to produce and appreciate rhythm, pitch, and timbre. • *Bodily-Kinesthetic*—ability to control one's body movements and to handle objects skillfully. • *Visual-Spatial*—capacity to think in images and pictures, to visualize abstractly and accurately.
Social	• When children use language for a real exchange of ideas and information among themselves. • A child says or does something that indicates a sense of humor. • A child appears to modify his or her language for less mature children. • When a child behaves in a way that indicates sensitivity to the needs or feelings of another child who had fallen or might move out of the way of another child without being asked.	• *Interpersonal*—capacity to detect and respond appropriately to the moods, motivations, and desires of others. • *Intrapersonal*—capacity to be self-aware and in tune with inner feelings, values, beliefs, and thinking processes.

(continued)

Table 2.1. (*continued*)

Gifts and Talents among Children	Identification	Multiple Intelligences
	• A child uses verbal skills to handle conflict or to influence other children's behavior.	
Interests	• When a child loves to learn new things and expresses a curiosity about many things. He or she spends most of his or her free time drawing, reading, and seeking out new information on whatever the topic may be. • Notice when a child becomes totally absorbed in one kind of knowledge. • Notice when a child displays great interest or skill in ordering and grouping items. • Notice when a child is unusually attentive to features of the classroom environment.	• *Musical*—ability to produce and appreciate rhythm, pitch, and timbre. • *Naturalist*—ability to recognize and categorize plants, animals, and other objects in nature. • *Visual-Spatial*—capacity to think in images and pictures, to visualize abstractly and accurately. • *Bodily-Kinesthetic*—ability to control one's body movements and to handle objects skillfully.
Abstract Thinking	• The child may have an understanding of abstract or complex ideas. • The child may be able to express an understanding of abstract concepts such as death, time, or electricity. The child can discuss these concepts appropriately and in context. • Notice when a child displays skills putting together new or difficult puzzles, particularly examining the shape of puzzle pieces and seeming to know where to place them without trial and error. • Notice when a child spontaneously makes up songs or stories. • Notice when a child uses metaphors or analogies.	• *Existential*—sensitivity and capacity to tackle deep questions about human existence, such as meaning of life, why we die, and how we get here. • *Mathematical-Logical*—ability to think conceptually and abstractly.

Source: The table is adopted from: Roedell, W. C., Jackson, N. E., & Robinson, H. B. (1980). *Gifted Young Children*. New York: Teachers College Press.

SUMMARY

- The basics of child development could be categorized in four different domains: physical, social, cognitive, and emotional.
- Physical development can be divided into two categories: gross motor and fine motor development.
- Erikson (1950) identified eight universal stages of human development. The first four stages address the early years: (1) Trust vs. Mistrust, (2) Autonomy vs. Shame and Doubt, (3) Initiative vs. Guilt; and (4) Identify vs. Confusion.
- It is important for adults to speak with children in a positive manner. They should explain and rationalize appropriate behavior, but avoid telling children what "not" to do. If a child exhibits socially inappropriate behavior, adults should redirect the child's attention in positive ways that help the child cope with his or her anger or emotions. Finally, it is important to focus on children's strengths, and work with them to improve weaknesses.
- Children learn from experience. It is important for teachers and parents to provide the best experiences possible through field trips, visits, and travel.
- Children learn differently and the way they learn varies based on their age and stage of development.
- It is important to identify a child's gifts and talents.

Thinking Questions

1. How would you help children to grow and learn in today's world?
2. Prioritize the learning practices that you will adopt for your children's development.

REFERENCES

Bell, L. C., & Perfetti, C. A. (1994). Reading skill: Some adult comparisons. *Journal of Educational Psychology*, 86, 244–255.

Caulfield, R. (2000). Number matters: Born to count. *Early Childhood Education Journal*, *28*(1), 63–65.

Copple, C., & Bredekamp, S. (2009). *Developmentally appropriate practice in early childhood programs serving children from birth through age 8* (3rd ed.). National Association for the Education of Young Children.

Engel-Smothers, H., & Heim, S. M. (2009). *Boosting your baby's brain power.* Scottsdale, AZ: Great Potential Press, Inc.

Erikson, E. H. (1950). *Childhood and society.* New York: Vintage.

Frey, N., & Fisher, D. (2010). Reading and the brain: What early childhood educators need to know. *Early Childhood Education, 38,* 103–110.

Gardner, H. (1983). *Frames of mind: The theory of multiple intelligences.* New York: Basic Books.

Gesell, A., & Ilg, F. (1949). *Child development.* New York: Harper.

Hart, B., & Risley, T. R. (1999). *The social world of children learning to talk.* Baltimore: Paul H. Brookes.

Hebb, D. O. (1949). *The organization of behavior.* New York: Wiley.

LaBerge, D., & Samuels, S. J. (1974). Toward a theory of automatic information processing in reading. *Cognitive Psychology, 6*(2), 293–323.

Maslow, A. H. (1943). A theory of human motivation. *Psychological Review, 50*(4), 370–96. Retrieved from http://psychclassics.yorku.ca/Maslow/motivation.htm.

Medina, J. (2008). *Brain rules: 12 principles for surviving and thriving at work, home, and school.* Seattle: Pear Press.

Piaget, J. (1954). *The construction of reality in the child.* New York: Basic Books.

Siegler, R. S. (2000). *Childhood cognitive development: The essential readings.* Malden, MA: Blackwell.

Skinner, B. F. (1938). The behavior of organisms: an experimental analysis. Oxford: Appleton-Century.

Slegers, B. (1997, April 17). Brain development and its relationship to early childhood education. Paper presented at EDEL 695 Seminar in Elementary Education, Long Beach, CA.

Squire, L. R., & Kandel, E. R. (2000). *Memory: From mind to molecules.* New York: W. H. Freeman.

Vygotsky, L. (1930). *The socialist alteration of man,* in van Der Veer, R., and Vasliner, J., Eds. (1998). *The Vygotsky Reader,* Oxford: Blackwell.

Wasserman, L. H. (2007). The correlation between brain development, language acquisition, and cognition. *Early Childhood Education Journal, 34*(6), 415–418. doi: 10.1007/s10643-007-0155-x.

Watson, J. B. (1913). *Psychology as the behaviorist views it.* Psychological Review, 20 (2).

Chapter Three

Home, School, and Community Involvement in Children's Development

In order to be effective, schools must partner with families and communities. Educators should reach out to parents, families, and other community members and keep them involved (Warner & Curry, 1997). Such partnerships are necessary because children gain knowledge and develop a sense of belonging to their communities when families and communities actively work together. According to Gestwicki (2010), the rubric for creating and sustaining a comprehensive home-school-community partnership program should be tailored to individual communities.

Even though individual communities differ to a certain extent, most communities exhibit similar traits. School, which is a part of the community, has multiple functions. It acts as a bridge between family and the community at large. The nurturance that children receive is mainly from home and the school. It is important for teachers to realize that parents know their children best. Parents prefer child-centric programs that are rewarding from both academic and non-academic perspectives and held in comfortable and appropriate settings. Programs should cultivate environments that are safe and conducive to learning.

Before the child enters preschool, the child understands the world through his or her family first. Bronfenbrenner's Ecological Theory in figure 1 explains this point further by noting that a child's worldview consists of five systems: Microsystem, Mesosystem, Exosystem, Macrosystem, and lastly Chronosystem. Starting from the center of the figure and moving out, one can see that a child's first interaction is with his or her family, followed by school and peers. Their religious affiliations, parent's workplace, and neighborhoods also influence children.

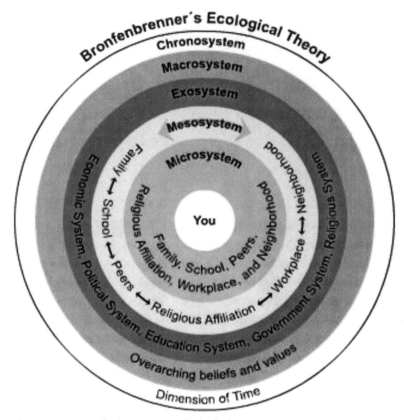

Figure 3.1. Bronfenbrenner's Ecological Theory

HOME INFLUENCE

From infancy, children are exposed to their caregivers and relatives; thus, the importance of the home in a child's life is obvious. At home, children learn different ways to be heard and understood—that is, through cooing or crying. They learn the home language and the culture even before their first baby step. When both parents work, infants start going to day care and learn to adjust to a different culture and community from their first day. They get used to the routine slowly and it often becomes a part of their lives. Building partnerships with the preschool community may facilitate transitions for children. Both can keep each other posted. A healthy partnership between parents and teachers only benefits the child.

While teachers are knowledgeable about child development, parents may be specialized in other fields. Parents often have specialized knowledge that can contribute to enriching classroom instruction. The enrichment will benefit not only their children, but also their children's peers. Parents might be doctors, nurses, lawyers, political figures, and so on. Parents with special expertise may enrich the classroom experience for all children.

Furthermore, diverse families could bring their own expertise from their own countries. Parents could share their knowledge with the school community to enrich classroom experience. To extend this knowledge further, parents could also take their children to various countries to expose them to different cultures, languages, and customs. Travel broadens children's thinking and inspires them; it also encourages them to meet interesting people and form connections with others. After and during visits, children could keep journals in which they recount travel stories and paste pictures they've taken.

Additionally, family members and relatives may contribute a great deal to help the child grow. Grandparents, in particular, play a big role in child development. With their experience and wisdom, grandparents become advisors and advocates for their grandchildren. Children without grandparents are deprived of much in life. Grandparents provide a special type of love and warmth for grandchildren, which is very important for children's emotional development. This is especially true for children living with single parents. Grandparents become friends, philosophers, and guides to grandchildren.

Given the important support parents and grandparents provide children, it is important to note that homeless children, who are often deprived of parents and grandparents, need extra special attention. Teachers of homeless children thus play double or triple roles in their lives. In many cases, homeless children develop negative self-perceptions that impact them from a developmental standpoint; in these cases, teachers have a responsibility to show more love and affection for those children. In the absence of significant home influences, it is important to note that schools and communities play relatively larger roles in the lives of homeless children.

SCHOOL INFLUENCE

Like home influence, school climate plays a big role in a child's life. How to adjust in a group, how to share toys with friends, how to take turns, how to learn negotiation skills—all of these skills are reinforced in school. Thus, teachers are responsible for teaching children how to socialize and build communities. School is a place in the community where children build academic and non-academic skills.

To teach academic and non-academic skills to children, teacher preparation is a key factor; preparation differs from country to country. For example, teacher preparation in France is intense and helps educators to truly be multidisciplinary. They spend a lot of time studying and preparing for the competitive exam for teaching. In Finland, students in the college or university earning a *cum laude* or *summa cum laude* are generally teachers. On the other hand, teachers adopt the role of mother in Italy, so the schools are known as *scuola maternal*, meaning the maternal school. Interestingly, in France, school principals are supposed to manage the administration and serve as a colleague by teaching in the classroom. Principals spend certain days of the week in the classroom and certain days managing the school. Therefore, in different countries, teachers and principals have important roles to play in the children's lives.

It is suggested that along with academic knowledge, children need to be exposed to hands-on learning experiences. Schools should take children on a field trip before the end of every unit. Through field trips, children acquire firsthand knowledge, and learning becomes more interesting because they can relate better to the content of their study. Besides academic enrichment, children enjoy taking trips because it gives them a significant amount of time out of their routines and offers new experiences.

FIELD TRIP IDEAS

Parents can take their children to visit different places or to different countries.

Parents or teachers could take the children on trips to public libraries, museums, educational shows, seasonal celebrations, holiday celebrations, festivals, etc.

School days are structured differently in other countries. In China, for example, school starts at about 7 a.m. and ends at 7 p.m. That may seem like a long day, but children learn academics in the morning, followed by lunch. In the afternoon, they engage in enrichment programs, which are followed by non-academic teaching. They have a choice of music programs, sports activities, art classes, and various other types of extracurricular activities. After 7 p.m., parents take their children home and have dinner together. Homework and enrichment, activities typically done at home in an American household, are taken care of at schools in China.

While homework maintains continuity between school and home, educators should make sure children are not overburdened with work. Assignments should be stimulating and reinforce work done at school; at the same time, the work should be fun for children, and something they can complete independently. Currently, homework in U.S. schools is increasingly becoming more work for the parents and creating unnecessary pressure for children. In an average American household, a child goes to school around 8 a.m. and returns home around 5 or 6 p.m. Given this schedule, children are left little time to complete their assignments. Some may feel overwhelmed; this, in turn, decreases their capacity to learn from homework, and generally makes them more disinterested in schoolwork. In addition, often the assignments that are given do not stimulate children enough; worksheets, for example, often require a regurgitation of information.

Homework should provide children with opportunities to learn and proactively apply new knowledge. For example, in many cases, reading a book or solving math problems would be more beneficial assignments for children than worksheets. Educators should strive to create a balance in the kinds of assignments they give. Occasional worksheets benefit children when they have an adequate understanding of the material; without such an understanding, children grow frustrated with assignments, and their self-esteem suffers.

It is also important for educators to strive for a better balance in the school environment, between academic and non-academic programs. One quick way of doing this in schools in the United States is to build effective after-school programs, where students can work on homework while enjoying creative outlets in the form of music, art programs, and sports activities. It is possible to incorporate all of these elements in after-school programs.

A meta-analysis of *after-school* programs that seek to enhance the personal and social skills of children and adolescents indicates that participants in after-school programs demonstrated significant increases in their self-perception and bonding to *school*, as well as increased positive social behaviors, *and* levels of academic achievement, and significant reductions in problem behaviors. (Durlak, Weissberg, & Pachan, 2010). Therefore, while schools try to wear different hats, effective after-school programs can create an effective bridge between school and family.

COMMUNITY INFLUENCE

Community plays a big role in a child's life. Although schools are part of communities, they need the support of the community in order to thrive. Thus, schools and different agencies within communities should cultivate partnerships that allow communal resources and expertise to be accessible to schoolchildren. After-school programs could be these bridges between communities and schools.

BUILDING AN EFFECTIVE PROGRAM

Building an effective after-school program allows children to learn in relaxed environments, where they enjoy themselves as they perform various tasks. An effective after-school program provides both academic and non-academic enrichment. Furthermore, remaining within the school building gives children a secure environment.

The main objective of after-school programs is to develop the "whole child" by nurturing the following dimensions of development: physical, cognitive, emotional, and social. Along with academic knowledge, children also need to be exposed to the arts and music. Sports, puzzles, and games facilitate teamwork and sharpen children's competitive edges. They allow children to learn and to interact with others and form new partnerships. Finally, they can be used as excellent learning tools because they teach children lessons they wouldn't normally learn within the classroom.

CHILDREN FROM DIVERSE BACKGROUNDS

Rodriguez-Brown (2008) offers a critique of family literacy programs in culturally and linguistically diverse communities. Literacy programs

Family Field Trips

must have a clear design for literacy activities relevant to community goals. He offers an alternative literacy model that is grounded in an abiding respect for parents as their children's first, and ultimately, most important teachers.

In U.S. schools, children from diverse cultural and linguistic backgrounds are steadily increasing. It is important to realize that families with different ethnic backgrounds could enrich after-school programs. Oftentimes, different cultural experiences can make families resourceful in different areas. If teachers are unaware of diverse cultures, parents should be invited to step in. Parents could offer their help in this respect. In that way a child coming from a different background would not feel isolated.

BUILDING AN EFFECTIVE SUMMER PROGRAM

It is also important to consider the summer months. For two months, children are out of school, and studies show that the progress they make in school declines as a result of the time they have off. Although most schools insist that children should develop a habit of reading daily, effective summer programs could play an important role in stimulating and maintaining children's progress.

Creating a Summer Program

The following is an example of an effective summer program that could be created:

"Learn while you play and play while you learn" is the motto of an effective summer program.

The program could function using a theme-based approach: each week, children work on different themes. Children engage in creative activities that are grade specific. This approach involves an integrated curriculum where children learn and improve their reading, writing, math, and science skills, and engage in arts and crafts. They learn a foreign language, play games, and solve puzzles according to their respective age and grade level.

Example: Week 1: Theme: Food & Nutrition (other weeks will have different themes: Environment, Solar System, etc.).

Reading	Children will learn about the food pyramid, and read books on healthy food and nutrition (knowledge).
Writing	Each child will be encouraged to draw or write on the specific food/nutrition topic that he or she plans to choose (improve vocabulary and writing skills).
Poetry	Children will create a poem on a chosen topic and publish it (literary skills and self-confidence).
Math	Age-appropriate math activities including recipes, ingredients (e.g., fractions, weight, measurement, etc.) (intellectual ability and cognitive skills).
Science	Age-appropriate, hands-on science activities (e.g. proteins, carbohydrates, effects on human health; reasons for eating carrots? . . . a good source of Vitamin A, etc.) (inquiry-based learning).
Computer	Children will utilize computer skills to draw, write, and label objects. Find resources and pictures from the Internet (cognitive, fine motor skills, and eye-hand coordination).

Arts & Crafts	Children will use a variety of drawing and craft materials in a structure that ensures a sense of accomplishment and freedom that permits individuality and creative expression (visual learning, creativity, and fine motor skills).
Music	Children learn various songs related to food and nutrition (cognitive skills, attention, harmony, and internal order).

Outcome of the Week

Children create nutrition bags in class, and bring them home to share what they've learned with parents. Critical thinking skills improve as children narrate the topic, address its salient points, and give their perspective on its significance. Children also learn Spanish words related to this unit (improving language skills).

Likewise, each week's instructions relate to a specific theme with hands-on activities for children.

Schools during school hours have the responsibility of teaching to specific standards and focusing on students' development of academic skills. In this context, teachers find it difficult to offer non-academic enrichment to students. Furthermore, school budgets hardly permit schools to offer a wide range of activities, such as music, art, or sports, which are absolutely essential for child development. Hence, schools should incorporate non-academic activities into after-school programs.

ACTIVE PLAY IN AFTER-SCHOOL PROGRAMS

Active play is associated with children's physical activity; hence, *after-school* programs can potentially offer critical experiences. Strategies to promote active play may prove to be a successful means of increasing children's physical activity (Brockman, Jago, & Fox, 2010). Therefore, non-academic parts should be built into the program so that students get physical activity.

In sports, children will be grouped according to their grades. They will develop gross motor skills and fine motor skills for individual sports like tennis. They will also participate in team sports such as basketball and soccer. Playing in groups will allow children to learn team building, while also helping them to improve individual skills that build and reinforce their focus and attention.

The "music and movement" session will add a unique dimension to the program. It focuses on accuracy and attention. Music uses an inherent structure to reinforce a sense of internal order. It will connect a particular vocal sound or tune of the instrument with a specific body movement, and provides more than one neural pathway by using multisensory channels. Children will utilize their visual, auditory, and kinesthetic attributes. The program will focus on deeper psychological processes and allow creative expressions of the children, and will challenge gifted students to adapt their existing abilities in ways that enable them to produce musical notes.

It is important to teach our children to develop coordination, enhance body awareness, and explore ways to communicate through cooperative physical exercises. Children will develop greater self-confidence while reinforcing the concept of art forms as a medium of communication through dance. Children will engage in movement games that build spatial awareness and group cooperation. Furthermore, in an adaptation of this program, we will engage children in an exploration of dance as it is used in different cultures, both artistically and socially (improving emotional, physical, and social skills). Associating arts with math and science and with music benefits children holistically.

Further, after-school programs benefit children by offering time for free play. This helps children feel relaxed and refreshed. It also helps foster creativity and imagination among children. Below is an example of a child who had initiated an imaginary concept of a store and had all the other children get involved in it. Following is a write-up from the child (age nine) who initiated the concept of the store.

Children's Creation of their Own Play Activity

THE STORE

"THE STORE" is an activity in an after-school program. As founder and manager of the "THE STORE," I must say that our customers, workers, and everybody else involved in this activity offers a great deal of help by working extremely hard, cleaning up after the store is closed, and giving their utmost support.

In "THE STORE," what we basically do is sell paper knickknacks. We use origami to make such items. We also mount children's artwork on construction paper for that purpose. For example, we sell paper swans, penguins, frogs, airplanes, mice, cups, ninja stars, etc. In exchange for our paper toys, we get fake paper money. However, we only accept the paper money made by one of the worker's own hands. The way to earn our fake paper money is to do good deeds like helping people with homework, cleaning up after one's mess, having stupendous behavior, etc. The customers then use their fake paper money to purchase paper objects from "THE STORE."

Our beloved store was created for one reason. It was made to add more fun to the program than it already has. However, as "THE STORE" got more customers and got larger, I have realized that "THE STORE" isn't just about fun, but it is also about the community. It helps the young children of today realize what it would be like to shop in a store in the future. It also gives the workers a chance to learn how people who work in actual stores work and handle business. So, in conclusion, "THE STORE" is not only for entertainment, but also for giving experience.

THE PROGRAM STRENGTHENS HOME, SCHOOL, AND COMMUNITY

The program should not only connect but also should strengthen home, school, and community. After-school teachers help children who are having a hard time in school. Field trips in the community could be taken to the public library, the New York Hall of Science, Alley Pond Environmental Center, and the zoo. Personnel from the local fire department could be invited to come to the school and speak to the children about fire safety.

They usually bring in the fire truck to show how a fire is extinguished. The children could get a chance to see the inside of the fire engine. The officers from the neighborhood bank could be invited to come to talk to the children about how to save money and have bank accounts. They usually speak to the children about how to deposit money in the account.

Schools and the community can work together to create programs for children. The community could organize art exhibitions, festivals, cultural program seasonal events, and science fairs for the children in respective schools.

If school, home, and community bondage is strong then it certainly benefits children. School, home, and community are interrelated, and their relationship is reciprocal. Certainly, each of the above can operate on its own, but children will be deprived the most if the school, home, and community are not together. The experience that young minds get in their childhood years stays forever. It leaves an impact that hopefully the children will give back to the bigger community by being good citizens.

SUMMARY

- Children are influenced from home, school, and the community.
- A great deal of influence on children comes from home/parent interactions and family relationships that contribute to help the child grow. A healthy partnership between parents and teachers benefits the child. Parents with expertise in their fields and culture could also contribute to enrich the classroom instruction, which will benefit the whole class.
- Teachers need to take an active step to learn the culture of their students. In that way a child coming from a different background would not feel isolated.
- School is a place in the community where children build academic and non-academic skills.
- Although school is a part of the community, it needs support from the rest of the community; for instance, different agencies that are in the community can bring resources and expertise to schoolchildren.
- After-school programs and summer programs may be used to connect schools and the community.

Thinking Questions

1. What are the influences of home, school, and community on the children?
2. Develop a project to help children understand the strength of home, school, and community relationships.
3. List all the places that you can take your children. Estimate the amount of money and anticipate the learning outcome for each place of interest.

REFERENCES

Brockman, R., Jago, R., & Fox, K. R. (2010). The contribution of active play to the physical activity of primary school children. *Preventive Medicine, 51*(2), 144–147.

Durlak, J. A., Mahoney, J. L., Bohnert, A. M., & Parente, M. E. (2010). Developing and improving after-school programs to enhance youth's personal growth and adjustment. *American Journal of Community Psychology, 45*(3/4), 285–293.

Durlak, J. A., Weissberg, R. P., & Pachan, M. (2010). A meta-analysis of after-school programs that seek to promote personal and social skills in children and adolescents. *American Journal of Community Psychology, 45*(3/4), 294–309.

Gestwicki, C. (2010). *Home, school, and community relations* (7th ed.), Wadsworth Cengage Learning.

Rodriguez-Brown, F. V. (2008). *The home-school connection: Lessons learned in a culturally and linguistically diverse community*. Taylor and Francis.

Roth, J, L., Malone, L.M., & Brooks-Gunn, J. (2010). Does the amount of participation in afterschool programs relate to developmental outcomes? A review of the literature. *American Journal of Community Psychology, 45* (3/4), 310–324.

Warner, C., & Curry, M. (1997). *Everybody's house—the schoolhouse: Best techniques for connecting home, school, and community*. London: Sage Publications.

Chapter Four

Understanding Young Children through Observation, Documentation, and Assessment of Behavior

Observation, which involves looking at something over time and in different contexts, is a useful mechanism for identifying behaviors among children. Teachers and researchers observe children in their various "natural" settings—in their homes, child-care centers, schools, and other communal areas—to collect raw, descriptive data on them. Researchers then categorize, sort, and interpret data to suggest overarching patterns in children's behaviors.

Teachers with experience develop different observation techniques. The great advantage of observation over other forms of assessment of young children is that it is nonintrusive and does not disturb the children's routine. It is vitally important to children's well-being that teachers become accomplished observers, because it allows them to determine how each child is developing and learning at optimal levels.

Teachers play a critical role in the observation process, and have two key responsibilities. First, teachers should conduct periodic observations to track children's progress. Second, teachers must appraise their own practices in the classroom and tailor them to the developmental needs of children. Observation gives them the general overview they need to make changes to curricula, and helps them analyze and address specific classroom management problems.

Parents and caretakers could keep a learning log of their children's accomplishments. Teachers should also make a point of adding their written observations on individual children to other information they share with study teams, parents, and administrators. It is important to remember to protect the confidentiality of children, so it is important to be as unobtrusive as possible. Below are some sets of guidelines that a teacher might need to know:

A GUIDELINE FOR OBSERVATION FOR TEACHERS

- Who will be observed?
- What behavior(s) will you observe?
- How will you observe the behavior(s)?
- When will you observe?
- How will you document your observations?
- How will you use the information that you have obtained?

TIPS FOR TEACHERS BEFORE DOING ANY OBSERVATION

- While each school district must follow the code of ethics that its state government has adopted, early childhood teachers have their own code of ethics.
- Become familiar with the school's philosophy and rules.
- Make a name tag for yourself if you are a student teacher.
- The teacher should position himself/herself to meet a child's level by sitting down.
- Encourage children to talk out loud while they complete tasks. Write down what they say.
- If disciplinary matters arise, try teaching children negotiating skills.
- Take time to listen to children. Be a good listener.
- Be sensitive to the appropriate use of touching and holding in all situations.
- Be prepared to supervise outdoor, as well as indoor, activities. Negligence on duty may result in a legal case.
- Anticipate what needs to be done.
- As much as possible, focus on how children are doing, rather than on your own performance.
- Comply with any medical regulations.

PURPOSE OF OBSERVATION

The main purpose of observation is to allow teachers to identify children's needs and interests. In order to fulfill the purpose of doing observations, teachers should chart the developmental level of each child, because such knowledge assists them in planning appropriate academic curricula based on individual needs and allows them to appraise their own teaching practices and design appropriate staff trainings. Observation can give practitioners a general overview of their own programs, while helping them analyze and address specific classroom management problems.

In short, we have to figure out how to observe a child, work with a child, and then develop a relevant curriculum. Observations help provide a richer picture of a child's development over time. In this way, observation helps us notice children better and catch things that we would otherwise miss. Finally, it is a tool that gives us a fresh perspective on our routines and aspects of our environment, such as room arrangement and curricular materials, and of course to know the needs of the child better.

FREQUENCY OF OBSERVATION

Teachers should conduct daily observations to determine children's progress. During observation, they should also make a point of keeping a notepad and pen readily available. Through a travel abroad program, the author of this book travels with a group of teachers to Italy and France. In Italy, for example, teachers always carry a notepad and a pen in their apron pockets because they always want to be prepared to make notes of interesting behaviors. Written observations are important because they supplement other information and can be shared with study teams, parents, and administrators.

Observation is beneficial for several reasons. It allows teachers to anticipate what needs to be done in the curriculum and if any change is necessary in the environment. A careful, unbiased observation helps unravel the mysteries and answers to some of the unanswered questions about children's behavior. Looking closely at the observations helps teachers to interpret behavior and plan accordingly. Observation and interpretation should be kept separate in teacher notes. Observation notes list factual information—a record of what one sees—whereas interpretation is more judgmental. Teachers should note this and be cautious of biases that may be embedded in their own observations of children; such biases lead to hasty and often incorrect judgments of children.

DIFFERENT FORMS OF DOCUMENTING OBSERVATION

The two main forms of documenting observations are narrative and non-narrative. Among narrative forms of documentation are running records, anecdotes, and ABC narratives. Non-narrative forms of documentation include checklists and rating scales.

Running records: A running record is a continuous observation and record of a behavior at a certain time. A well-written running record is a rich description of a naturally occurring behavior. This is particularly useful when students show evidence of disruptive or problematic behaviors because it allows the teacher to note the context and times in which the behaviors occur.

Anecdotal records: An anecdote is a brief story of an important developmental event. Like a story, an anecdote has a beginning, middle, and end. It can also contain many other elements of a story in that it usually describes a specific setting, lays out a record of events in a sequential manner, and provides a solution to a problem, or a resolution at the end. An anecdotal record is an open narrative, and a brief form of observation that early childhood teachers like to use to record a child's developmental progress. In this way, it is essentially a snapshot of a child's development in the classroom. These anecdotal records are particularly helpful when trying to give parents a picture of their child's classroom participation and work. They also help provide individual portraits of children that capture both their individual abilities and ways that they work in groups.

ABC narrative: The ABC narrative event sampling method investigates what precedes (the antecedents) and what follows (the consequences) a behavior.

A—Antecedents
B—Behavior
C—Consequences

Checklist: A checklist is a list of characteristics or behaviors that an observer marks off if they are present with a check mark. Checklists are primarily used to assess the current characteristics of an observational subject (child, teacher, curriculum, or environment) and also to track changes in these characteristics over time. It is an effective way of determining the presence or absence of behaviors.

Rating scales: A rating scale is an observational tool that indicates the degree to which a person possesses a certain trait or behavior; it is often a list of characteristics or activities. It shows how much of something is observed, and is therefore another way for teachers to summarize observations and make judgments about a child's regular performance. Rating scales help teachers organize information in a quick and orderly way. When a teacher wants to note the extent to which a child exhibits a behavior or completes a task, rating scales are useful. They can also be utilized when teachers want to demonstrate progressions or gradations in the data.

It is highly suggested that teachers try each protocol out in class for five minutes and then share the findings with other teachers, and talk about which protocols are most useful and why.

OUR RESPONSIBILITY TO ALL CHILDREN

It is important to observe all children in their natural settings—while they are playing or working. In order to truly help children reach developmental goals, both parents and teachers need to observe and keep records of their observations of children, and take care to note dates and times, as well as provide supplemental materials, such as photographs or videos. All observations should be included in a portfolio that tracks a child's development. These long-term, detailed records are ultimately useful, because they allow us to better serve children with developmental needs and become better advocates on their behalf.

SUMMARY

- The main purpose of observation is that it allows teachers to identify children's needs and interests. This assists educators in planning appropriate curricula based on the needs of individual children.

- Teachers should also conduct periodic observations to track children's progress.
- Teachers should have notepads and pens readily available for observations.
- Teachers should maintain portfolios for individual children that contain their notes from observations, students' work/projects, exams, photographs, and/or videos that document children's progress.

Thinking Questions

1. How can observation and documentation help teachers to understand and assess children's behavior?
2. Observe and document the behavioral aspect of children in their social interactions within the school environment.

Chapter Five

Curriculum Development and the Role of the Environment in Education

As parents, teachers, and teacher-educators, we aspire to foster a lifelong love of learning among children. This is only possible when children are in safe environments—spaces that nurture their learning potential and stimulate their minds. Thus, one of our primary responsibilities is to construct such spaces.

PLAY-BASED LEARNING

Importance of Play

Throughout the world, play is recognized as an important learning tool (Riley, San Juan, Klinker, & Ramminger, 2008). It helps children develop self-regulation and promotes language, numeracy, and social skills. During play, children actively participate in integrated activities, often solving complex dilemmas. Because of its importance, play should be facilitated by teachers and educators in well-designed environments. As one study notes, the environment "is the backdrop to play, supplying content, context, and meaning" (Cosco & Moore, 1999).

Theoretical Framework of Play

Froebel (1912), the father of kindergarten, stated, "Play is the highest expression of human development in childhood for it alone is the free expression of what is in the child's soul." Thus, play is one of the main ways children express meaning. Vygotsky (1930) posited that play serves sev-

41

eral additional purposes, as well. First, play encourages abstract thought by separating meanings from objects; for example, during play, a child may imagine a building block into a telephone to call daddy. Second, play allows learning to be supported or encouraged by other competent peers. Third, play encourages self-talk, which leads to greater self-regulation (Johnson, Christie, & Wardle, 2005).

Play is important in children's lives. Piaget (1962) describes three stages of play. The first stage (birth to age two) consists of practice sensorimotor play, which is characterized by repetition; children repeatedly practice the same activity. For example, a toddler may continually fill up a bucket with sand and then empty it out again and again. The second stage is symbolic play (ages two to seven). Piaget writes that, in this stage, children begin to use symbols, a sign of intellectual development. Piaget further divides this stage into three subtypes: constructive play (creating and inventing play with materials), dramatic play (engaging in pretend play), and socio-dramatic play (pretending to play with other children). The third stage is games with rules (ages seven to eleven) such as board games and card games. Piaget emphasizes the complementary processes of accommodation and assimilation during this stage. As he describes it, accommodation is "the modification of internal schemes to fit reality" and assimilation is "the filtering or modification of the input." The latter is relevant to play; Piaget characterizes play as a pure form of the assimilative aspect of intellectual development.

Furthermore, as children play they are able to enter or depart from play frames. "Play frame" is the imaginative situation that children are involved in during play. Sigmund Freud (1915) argued that children become interested in play because of their need to deal with conflicts. He observed that play provides catharsis to children, as well as the opportunity to clarify and master their emotions; in essence, Freud saw play as therapy. Similarly, according to Erikson (1963) play substitutes for unfulfilled wishes and offers children a method for finding relief from traumatic events in their pasts. For example, a young girl punishes her doll for an imagined transgression just as her parents punish her. However, in the words of Bruner (1983), "Unless we bear in mind that play is a source of pleasure, we are really missing the point of what it is all about." In his book *The Hurried Child*, David Elkind (1988) categorizes play as a central part of children's early experience. Thus, teachers and educators should emphasize it, rather than "hurrying" children into the responsibilities and roles of older children.

Social Descriptions of play

Parten (1932) views play as a form of social interaction that facilitates and mirrors a child's growing ability to engage in cooperative actions with peers. The social descriptions of play as developed by Parten are as follows:

Unoccupied—the child is uninvolved in play.
Onlooker—the child watches others play.
Solitary—the child plays alone and avoids interacting with others.
Parallel—the child plays near others but does not engage in conversation.
Associative—the child begins to play with other children.
Cooperative—the child plays in a group.

Parents and teachers should observe children in play (see chapter 4) and use their observations to create more play opportunities for them. For example, if children are engaged in parallel play, a teacher could make sure there were duplicate or similar items available so every child has the chance to be involved in some way.

Characteristics of Play

Play is voluntary. Some types of play require the active involvement of the participants. Further, play involves symbolic activity. It is free from external rules—instead, rules are determined by the players. Play focuses on the process rather than the product and is pleasurable (Bullard, 2013). The first signs of pretend play occur around eighteen months when a child pretends to enact something in his life like eating. He might try to feed his bear or pretend to feed himself. However, when a child bangs on or drops an object, that is object manipulation and not considered play. Elkonin (1977, 1978) describes play in preschool years as object oriented. In later years, play among older preschool or kindergarten children becomes more socially oriented. Around five years of age children could play with games.

Benefits of Play

To summarize, play is beneficial to children in a number of ways.

1. Play positively contributes to children's quality of life because it stimulates emotional development. Since children feel happy during play, they develop more positive outlooks. Further, the National Institute of Mental Health finds that "growth, development, health, and high levels of cognitive and affective functioning in children are all associated with continuous ongoing participation in actions and interactions that are full of pleasure and playfulness" (Litchenberg & Norton, 1972).
2. Play is therapeutic for children because it provides a personal catharsis to them; in other words, it represents an outlet for their emotions. Therefore, it is especially important for adults to create opportunities for children to engage in play that mimics reality, such as "housekeeping" and "family" play.
3. Play promotes intellectual development because through it children can express meaning. When children engage in pretend play with objects, they express ideas that transcend the objects. Thus, pretend play allows children to develop the capacity to think abstractly. Further, the roles, rules, and motivational support provided by the imaginary situation during play provide children with the skills they need to think at a higher level.
4. Play helps children learn the frames of social life; in the play frame, children sort out different roles and then practice these roles in various contexts. For example, as they pretend to be mothers, fathers, policemen, teachers, firefighters, or doctors, they exhibit knowledge of each of these particular persons' particular positions and roles within society.
5. Play enhances language development. Play with peers is crucially important to the development of a child's language skills. Children are highly motivated to pay attention to language they hear from their peers. Language learning is thus an important outcome of peer interaction.
6. Play enhances interpersonal communication and social development. As children play together with peers, they also learn how to convey and receive ideas from others, and further build and clarify concepts

while coordinating their own views with other children. Therefore, play among children is essentially a collaborative process.

7. Play helps children release extra energy. Children need to be physically active before they settle down for quiet activities. The National Association for the Education of Young Children therefore advises teachers and parents that "[c]hildren need planned alterations of active and quiet activities" (Bredekamp, 1987).

8. Play helps children to develop self-regulation. During play, children cannot act in any way they please, because games are often associated with rules that they must follow. This encourages self-discipline.

Play Prepares a Child for Later Learning and More Advanced Activities

1. Symbolism. In advanced play, children use objects and actions symbolically. If children do not have the right props, they merely invent or substitute them with something else. For example, a child uses a rectangular block and pretends it to be a telephone and calls daddy at work.

2. Complex activities with multiple themes. In advanced play, children engage in activities with multiple themes. These involve new people, toys, and ideas that extend from a main theme. For example, if a child is playing "family" and the "baby" suddenly becomes ill, the child may imagine the involvement of an ambulance or a doctor, thereby extending the theme that forms a more complicated whole.

3. Complex, multiple roles. In advanced play, children assume multiple roles. For example, a child may imagine herself as "mommy," who, in addition to going to work in the morning, comes home to tend to a sick child. The child may then become the doctor who treats the sick child, before returning to the original mommy role.

4. Extended time period. In advanced play children can assume different roles for longer periods of time. Furthermore, advanced play may last longer than a day; for example, a child may continue playing the same role over the course of multiple days. Therefore, in some instances, it may be appropriate for teachers and parents to plan extended activities that last longer than a day.

Role of Adults in Supporting Play

Adults play significant roles in creating opportunities for children to play. First and foremost, children should have enough time for play; thirty to forty minutes of uninterrupted play daily is highly recommended. Furthermore, they should help children find themes for play by using stories, field trips, and other activities in the classroom to generate ideas. When children disagree on themes for activities, adults should encourage them to find creative ways to merge their ideas. Adults can also help children, especially preschoolers, to plan their play by brainstorming activities and providing props. These props could be from different cultures and be unfamiliar to children. It is also important that adults observe and monitor play in order to ensure that children are developing skills, remaining safe, and engaging in peaceful activities. When disputes between children arise, adults should be on hand to resolve them. Adults should also ensure that every child is involved or engaged in play, and make a point to include shyer children who are reluctant to join their peers. In all of these ways, adults can unobtrusively facilitate play for children. Following are some guidelines that teachers could remember as part of classroom management techniques.

Establish suitable expectations
  • Set appropriate expectations for children.
  • Set limits: children should know which behaviors are acceptable (knocking over a block tower built by someone is unacceptable).
  • Classroom rules: these need to be fair, reasonable, and appropriate to the children's age and maturity (be gentle to your friends, use words when you have a problem, etc.).
Arrange and modify the environment
  • Shelves need to be at the children's height so that they can access materials and return them.
  • The environment should have abundant materials for children's use.
  • There should be an open area for whole group to meet.
  • The curriculum should provide time for quiet and loud activities throughout the day.

Demonstrate appropriate behavior
- *Show*—show children where and how to take care of the classroom.
- *Demonstrate*—demonstrate proper ways to arrange the manipulatives and toys.
- *Model*—practice the behavior you expect of the children.

Foster pro-social behavior and empathy
- Model behaviors that are caring, loving, and helping.
- Provide opportunities to engage children in helping and service to others.
- Teach cooperative living and learning.

PLAY IDEAS WITH PARENTS AND CHILDREN

Parents should also play with their children to strengthen the bond. It could be a game bought from the store like Tic Tac Toe, Snakes and Ladders, Scrabble, etc. Tic Tac Toe could teach children how to manipulate through obstacles, and Snakes and Ladders teaches children about the ups and downs of life. Scrabble, on the other hand, is helpful in vocabulary learning. Adults could also make up games like passing the parcel or hot potato. Another idea is to come up with "name, place, animal, or thing" on a certain letter, where both the parent and the child have to come up with words. Storytelling is also an effective idea that could be taken in turns by parent and child. Children generally like to play outdoors and parents could also get actively involved.

CURRICULAR FRAMEWORK

There are several ways to organize classroom activities to facilitate play and other important high-order activities. Each approach has its own particular emphasis.

Theme-Based Approach

The theme-based approach is based on an "integrated curriculum." Thematic units could use a multidisciplinary approach, emphasizing the development of the "whole child." This high-quality program creates a developmentally appropriate framework of education where all the needs of the child are met. A holistic view of development recognizes interrelations between multiple domains of youth adjustment, and gives attention to multiple, relevant factors within and outside of the lives of youths that affect development. It also examines the dynamic interplay between persons, program features, and other contexts over time in order to understand the active role youth play in affecting their own development (Durlak, Mahoney, Bohnert, & Parente, 2010).

Project-Based Approach

The project approach refers to a set of teaching strategies that enable teachers to guide children through in-depth studies of real-world topics. This approach to teaching and learning is based on a vision of children as active learners, holistic learners, and learners capable of inquiry. It emphasizes the importance of supporting children's curiosity, their intrinsic motivation to learn, their growing critical awareness of the world around them, and their eagerness to reflect on and communicate their experiences and knowledge.

Definition of the Project Approach

A project is defined as an in-depth investigation of a real-world topic worthy of children's attention and effort. In other words, the project approach can be defined as in-depth investigation of a subject that is meaningful for children. Project work is an interactive process that includes activities requiring the active participation of a small group or an individual. These activities are related with the fields of study that attract children's attention and are chosen by children themselves (Tuğrul, 2002). Some examples of projects include: organizing to put on a play, opening up a class store, and carrying out a project to benefit the community, such as raising awareness of the importance of recycling. Project-based education has a significant impact on children's development in the sense that it gives answers to the questions of what children should learn and what the most effective ways of teaching those topics are (Curtis, 2002; Tuğrul, 2002).

Projects are not meant to take the place of teaching skills directly, but rather to provide a meaningful context in which skills can be developed and applied.

Theoretical Framework Supporting Project-Based Learning

Studies indicate that project-based education has positive impacts on children's personality development (Dungi, Sebest, Thompson, & Young, 2002; Liebovich, 2000; Tuğrul, 2002), motor development (Kim et al., 2001), cognitive development (Helm & Katz, 2001; Katz & Chard, 2000; Kucharski et al., 2005), language development (Beneke, 2003; Currie, 2001; Dungi, Sebest, Thompson, & Young, 2002; Helm, 2003; Katz & Chard, 2000), social/emotional development (Dungi, Sebest, Thompson, & Young, 2002; Helm & Katz, 2001; Katz & Chard, 2000), and self-care abilities (Ho, 2001; Myler, 2003). Further, it is observed that language, science, and mathematical skills are more comprehensible to preschool children who have been given a project-based education (Aslan & Köksal Akyol, 2006; Curtis, 2002; MacDonell, 2007; Tuğrul, 2002).

From these studies, it is clear that the "project approach" is effective in that it is child-centered, preparing children for investigation, research, and critical thinking, and raising awareness of social problems. In short, the project-based approach supports all areas of development (Katz & Chard, 2000) and provides children with the opportunity to study freely in an environment enriched with stimuli. In addition, it supports the development of key personal, cognitive, language, and social/emotional development as well as self-care abilities. (See figures 5.1 and 5.2.)

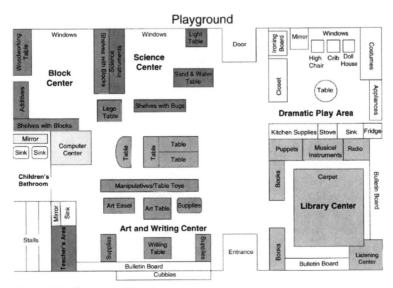

Figure 5.1. Classroom Map 1

Library Area

Sand and Water Center

Computer Center

The Loft

Listening Center

Math and Manipulatives Center

Figure 5.2. Classroom Map 2

Overview of the Phases of Project-Based Learning

Projects are structured in three phases. The phases are as follows:

Phase 1: During Phase 1, the teacher introduces a project topic to children. Often, the teacher will first plan a web of ideas for ways the project could develop. But throughout Phase 1, the teacher aims to have children reveal and share their previous experiences and knowledge related to the topic, to establish a sense of shared initial understanding of it, and to formulate questions that will allow them to explore the topic further. In this way, the teacher helps stimulate interest and curiosity about the topic and bases plans for future investigation on the interests and questions children already have. During Phase 1, teachers carefully listen to what children have to say about the topic, and provide children with opportunities to share their experiences with the topic through additional media besides conversation. Part of the documentation of Phase 1 will consist of quotes from children's initial discussion of the topic, as well as written stories and drawings depicting their experiences with it. In addition, teachers also usually create a topic web or list of questions with the children, known as an EKWQ (Experience, Knowledge, Wonder, and Questions). Often, the big challenge in this phase is finding successful strategies to get children to share their experiences and to come up with questions.

Phase 2: Sharing of and reflection on the group's previous experience with the topic is followed by the investigation phase. Based on interests revealed in Phase 1, the teacher has to plan for "fieldwork" that involves the class going on a field trip, and/or interviewing an expert on the topic, and/or filling the classroom with relevant objects, artifacts, and other "real-world stuff" related to the topic. A big challenge for teachers is deciding what primary sources they should draw on for this "real-world" investigation. Teachers often need to look further in their own community for helpful, relevant resources. Teachers can bring in experts from the community or ask for parental help if any parent is an expert in that field. Children prepare for "fieldwork" by formulating questions and researching the topic using secondary sources, such as photos, charts, and books. They also learn from each other. Children should be equipped with clipboards during the field investigation so they can jot down notes or make observational drawings. They should also be encouraged to discuss what they have experienced in the investigation and to represent their new knowledge in a variety of ways, including verbal presentations, writing, art media, dramatic plays, and various types of graphic organizers. Teachers should organize visual displays of this acquired knowledge in a way that allows children to reflect repeatedly on what they have experienced. When interest in a topic has peaked, and children have had an opportunity to express their learning in a variety of ways and to explore answers to their questions on the topic thoroughly, teachers should make plans for Phase 3.

Phase 3: This phase involves communicating, sharing, and presenting the work of the project to others who may be interested. This usually includes parents and other classes in the school. Children and their teachers should carefully select what to share and how to share it. During this phase, children may choose to personalize their new knowledge by creating stories, dramatic play sequences, and/or connecting with imaginative children's literature relevant to the topic.

How to Develop Project-Based Learning

Phase 1: Introduction Phase of a Project

Goals:

- Have children reveal and share previous experience and knowledge of the topic.
- Establish a sense of shared initial understanding of the topic.
- Get children to wonder about and create questions they wish to investigate about the topic.

Implementation:

- Teacher plans a tentative learning web.
- Teacher finds out what children have experienced and know.
- Teacher gets children to share their experiences.
- Teacher adapts his or her preliminary plans to take into account children's interests.

The main challenge is to get children to share experiences and to come up with questions.

Phase 2: Investigation Phase of a Project

- Based on interests revealed in Phase 1, plans are made for "fieldwork."
- This could involve a field trip, interviewing an expert guest, introducing into the room relevant objects and other "real-world" stuff children can use for hands-on investigation.

The challenge here is deciding what primary sources the teacher can draw upon for this "real-world" investigation.

Phase 3: Documentation Phase of a Project

Communicating, sharing, and presenting the work of the project to others who may be interested (usually parents and other classes in the school).

- Children and their teachers carefully select what to share and how to share it.
- Children personalize new knowledge by creating stories, dramatic play sequences.

The challenge is making children's thinking visible and showing what they learned and how it relates to learning standards.

Tips to Consider Before Starting Project-Based Learning

Start small with a simple topic.

Focus on a few key learning standards. Concentrate learning on one subject rather than multiple disciplines, because project-based learning emphasizes in-depth inquiry. Real-life fieldwork may be a good start but is not always necessary—learning can also occur in the classroom.

Plan the project with children. In project-based learning, teachers plan with children. They effectively map out a project with children in the classroom. Once this plan has been made, teachers can differentiate the instructions they give students to reflect the individualized learning needs of their classroom.

Technology tools can only aid the process.

When you first start project-based learning, focus on mastering the design and implementation process; technology can be used, but is not required.

There are studies that have found that project-based education is more effective than traditional methods (Ryser, Beeler, & McKenzie, 1995). In the traditional method, the teacher aims to develop children's skills; she selects the education environment and education materials herself, and is a specialist who is responsible for the success of the children. However, in the project approach, the teacher creates an environment for children to display their skills, presents different education environments and materials, and gives children the opportunity to customize their learning goals. In this way, project-based learning makes children the specialists in their own education. In this setting, the teacher uses her students' abilities while sharing in their success (Katz & Chard, 2000). Thus, the main difference between the two methods is that in the traditional method, the project itself represents learning. However, in project-based learning, the educator is teaching through the project.

Apart from the project-based approach, there are other approaches that allow teachers to explore teaching and learning with their students. Much has been written about the Reggio Emilia approach and Montessori approach in Italy. There is also the Agazzi approach to learning introduced by the Agazzi sisters.

In France, the National Ministry of Education recommends that preschool children learn through projects and the French education system recommends what the projects should be. This is consistent with several of the Italian methods of early childhood education that focus on projects.

In French preschools, children increase their language and vocabulary skills; they verbalize correct sentence structure and tell simple stories. Additionally, they learn to count, respect classroom rules, understand their body through physical education, and participate in painting and drawing exercises that help develop fine motor skills and prepare them for writing. Children also have the opportunity to move freely to express their feelings and to choreograph their own dance.

Similar to preschools in the United States, school days in France follow an organized structure. The following example was taken from observations made in a school in France. The teacher started the day with the calendar and weather. After that, the teacher introduced each activity that was going to take place in the centers. One activity was a board game where children had to roll dice to see what number and color counter they could place on their board. The children took turns and were respectful of each other. One child even helped her tablemate figure out the answer.

The school follows the national curriculum through projects. Specifically, the class I visited was doing a project based on the work of Monet, and the teacher—who also served the role of the principal of the school—took her children on a field trip to the mountains. After the trip, the children were asked to draw their experience with certain components of the trip, such as things they found on their nature walk, the sports they played, and the restaurant they ate in. After their drawings were completed, a small description of the drawing was also included.

Similar to France, Italy has public schools that are run by the state. In Italy, preschools are noncompulsory and are run by local municipalities. There are public and private schools in Italy.

The school is looked upon as a part of society for the child and family. The school is a welcoming place for all. The school also teaches moral values and it helps families to become aware of the needs and rights of children, no matter their social condition. The overall goal of the school is for children to work and do activities as a community.

Teachers have the responsibility to observe the everyday life of the child and provide spiritual and moral education. The materials used in the classroom are objects from everyday life such as yarn, buttons, images, etc., that children are familiar with. The Montessori method is often implemented, and it aims to self-develop and self-educate the child; the school should have the proper environment where the teacher can set up the environment and be a facilitator.

Usually there are no teacher desks in the classrooms. The materials used in the Montessori classrooms are usually for the individual child and are very specific, designed for one activity to reach a particular skill.

In addition to the Montessori and the Agazzi methods, there is also the Reggio Emilia approach. Loris Malaguzzi had a goal to create high-quality schools for all children in the city called Reggio Emilia. He had

study seminars in developing the educational approach and wanted to develop children through corners (centers) where there would be woodworking, puppetry, math, and long-term projects. There was also parental involvement early on to see if there were opportunities to enhance the curriculum and create extensions for the home. Hewett (2001) confirms that in the Reggio Emilia approach, "parents play an active role in ensuring that the early childhood education program their child attends is appropriate." Parents have the responsibility to mention any concerns they have about the curriculum. It is true that parent involvement is vital in the Reggio Emilia approach.

In Italy, educators want children to have a good relationship with nature. The children each have a symbol or an icon that is assigned to them (a common practice at several Italian schools) where they can easily locate their items. The icons are selected by the teacher and the child, and usually have the same number of syllables that the child's name has. Later on, the icons are replaced by children's names.

In the classroom, I observed a child who came in from the outside, went to her specific drawer, put an item away, proceeded to the bathroom, took a glass of water from the sink, put the empty glass in an area for dirty

glasses, and walked away. This child must have been no more than five years old and demonstrated autonomy and responsibility in her actions.

Like the French school, this Italian school also focused on projects. The specific project I viewed was on the painting *Angel* by Raphael. This was a project that took several months to complete, and the teacher had the children observe, draw pictures based on their experiences, and make their own portraits. The teacher was very proud of the students and saw growth in their ability to interpret art. She also saw growth in their fine motor skills.

In project-based learning, "The children have the opportunity to explore, observe, question, discuss, hypothesize, represent, and then proceed to revisit their initial observations and hypotheses in order to further refine and clarify their understandings" (Hewett, 2001). Teachers freely move around in the classroom and observe children when using the project method and it allows students to provide the teacher with feedback, which helps her to refine and adjust her plans accordingly.

This approach to learning will enhance the overall experience and creativity the children have with the project. This is similar to the description

New (1993) offers—that projects help children explore their experience with a topic, followed by problem solving with their peers, which provides opportunities for creative thinking and exploration.

Children who participated in the Reggio Emilia approach were involved in many creative activities where they used their imagination. They did this through painting, drawing, and participating in outside art. The work of the children is taken very seriously and, as stated by Hewett (2001), is respected; children are understood as having an innate desire to discover, learn, and make sense of the world.

At this particular school in Italy, there was extensive documentation of the children's experience with a particular project. This was evident throughout the school with projects being displayed throughout the building. It had pictures of the children as they wondered, asked questions, and participated in the project. There was also a description of the project and quotes from the children. It was wonderful to see how extensive this documentation was. Seitz and Bartholomew (2008) mentioned that documentation is defined as "samples of a child's work at several different stages of completion: photographs showing work in progress; comments written by the teacher or other adults working with the children; transcripts of children's discussions, comments, and explanations of intentions about the activity and comments made by parents."

Large portfolios are given to each of the parents with pictures of the child's work throughout the year. Each project has its own book with specific works of the child for the parents to review. This is similar to what was discussed by Seitz and Bartholomew (2008) in that portfolios can be made that show the specific progression of an individual child throughout the course of the project. Parents are also involved in their child's education and assist with specific projects such as creating a structure for the stained glass windows and watching the children as they attend a trip. Parental involvement with documentation is also stressed by Seitz and Bartholomew (2008) in that "parents can help teachers with documentation of the events of a specific project conducted in the classroom; some teachers may be in the process of gathering information on the work of the children and can collaborate with parents on how best to present it."

Maria Montessori's Philosophy

Maria Montessori's philosophy is based on a scientific view of children's learning (Gutek, 2004). According to Montessori (1989), educators and parents should encourage and promote independence among children. She advocated respect for children's needs as individuals to be independent and self-regulating. Children need to have choices to develop autonomy and positive self-esteem. Montessori mentioned recognition of the absorbent minds of the children and that children absorb knowledge directly from the environment. She emphasized that adults should pay attention to the sensitive periods of development among children. These times occur early in life, and during these times, children are susceptible to certain behaviors and can learn specific skills more easily. She warned that once the sensibility for learning a particular skill has occurred, it does not arise with the same intensity later on. Further, Montessori stressed the fact that children learn best from a prepared environment. She advocated for child-centered education and active learning. The three basic areas of child involvement begin with practical life that further builds concentration in motor activities and lengthens children's attention span—for example, polishing shoes, cleaning mirrors, watering plants, sweeping floors, dusting furniture, and peeling vegetables. The next area uses sensory materials, and the purpose is to train children's senses to focus on some obvious, particular quality—for example, to sharpen children's power of observation and increase their ability to think. The third area focuses on academic materials and the integration of reading and writing, as well as mathematics, using manipulatives that teach—for example, ten geometric forms, sandpaper letters, numerals, command cards, golden beads, and so on.

Reggio Emilia Approach

In the Reggio Emilia approach, children are portrayed as having one hundred "languages" (Malaguzzi, 1998), or expressive modes through which to demonstrate their understandings. Reggio Emilia teachers also believe that learning must be flexible and evolving; children's endeavors are purposeful if they connect past, present, and future. In the Reggio Emilia schools, a *pedagogista* serves as a mentor to teachers throughout the school year, reviewing their classroom documentation to help them plan emergent curricula. The child is viewed as a protagonist who is competent and full of ideas (Cadwell, 2003). The *pedagogista*s persuade educators to acknowledge the children's use of the visual arts as a "language," especially during project work. In Reggio art-based experiences are fundamental to children's learning. Reggio educators use documentation as a reflective tool for "making children's thinking visible," so their curriculum planning can follow the children's lead.

Agazzi Sisters' Teaching Philosophy

The Agazzi sisters believed that education comes from experience, and they centered the educational experience around the child. They further believed that schools should have a holistic vision of the child, and that the teachers must respect the natural rights of the child. They also believed that children learn through their senses and empower themselves through the environment. Thus, according to their approach, educators should observe, discover, and share with the children. This method was formed out of the needs of the students and utilized instruments, based on reality, that were appropriate to the particular environment, instead of using standardized measurements. During the time of the Agazzi sisters, the belief was that life must be simple and rational, and that material and physical order had a direct impact on moral order. This was very similar to Montessori's belief that the development of moral sense must serve as the basis for moral upbringing (Plekhanov, 1992).

A primary aspect of the Agazzi method was hygiene and care for the environment. Every morning, the teacher spent two-and-a-half hours on cleanliness. During Agazzi's time, the physical environment was difficult, as the school building had no heat, light, running water, or plumbing; the steps were too high; and the bathrooms were outside. Instead of being discouraged, the Agazzi sisters used this situation as a challenge. As an activity, for example, they had the children carry water in small buckets, and the children had to be careful not to spill any of the water. Since there was no heating, the children were taught to gather wood for fire. They were also responsible for washing chairs and tables. Space was limited, so the children were involved in learning how to reorganize their environment. The Agazzi sisters used these difficult situations as a means of teaching children to solve problems.

The basic notion of the method was simple and rational. The emphasis was to maintain physical order in order to impact moral order. This promoted the child's initiative and helped the child become responsible. This also implemented order in everything the child did, and thus helped establish order within each child. The children's work habits became part of their behavior. It helped children understand values and helped develop a moral sense, which ultimately resulted in the building of certain attitudes among the youngsters. This was based on the daily habits of the child, and their physical experiences.

Another characteristic of the Agazzi schools was the emphasis on the importance of physical activity in the education process. In other words, the school environment attempted to somewhat duplicate the home environment so that the children learned to follow rules. This method did not emphasize memory, but rather intellectualism. It was based on two kinds of play: guided play and free play. In this program, children were busy and active. Although each project had specific instructions, all activities had one common thread: respecting the educational environment.

Effective Practices in Early Childhood Education from Italy

The following tables compare the three different approaches to early childhood education. Tables 5.1 through 5.4 have been modified from the contribution made by M. Grazia Vinciguerra.

Learning Experience from One Municipal School Visit in Italy

Teachers participating in a travel abroad program had the pleasure of visiting a school in Italy. In general, the teachers design and implement teaching objectives by building on children's prior knowledge. This approach allows for both teacher-initiated and child-initiated learning experiences. A typical day in the program:

The School Environment

During the visit to the school, the most noticeable characteristic was the use of symbols on all of the children's items. Their cubbies, drawers, and work carried the same symbols, which the children recognized.

Table 5.1. Principles

Montessori	Agazzi	Reggio Emilia

• Respect for the child.
• Recognition of the absorbent mind of the child.
• Attention to sensitive periods of development.
• Recognition of self auto-education.
• Recognition of the importance of the role of the teacher.
• Children are encouraged to fulfill their spiritual, emotional, physical, and intellectual potential, as members of a family and a world community.
• Adults have the duty
  ∘ to respect individual differences
  ∘ to emphasize social interaction
  ∘ to educate the whole personality.
	• The child as a "vital seed aims at its own full growth" (Rosa Agazzi).
	• The child is an active person with his/her own growing potential that must be recognized, identified, and supported by the nursery school.
	• Children are naturally inclined to express themselves.
	• The school encourages their spontaneity, which is connected with family life (infant school) as an image of family.
	• Children do the same things they do at home.
		• The rights of the children are most important.
		• A child needs to feel secure and happy.
		• Everyone should have a right to live and get education.
		• The child is a part—in family, school, and society in general.
		• A child must wonder—a child has strength, imagination, and creativity that must be observed and applauded.
		• Participation of the parents is very important to the constitution of an educational process.

Table 5.2. Environment—Classroom (Mixed Ages, Learning from Each Other)

Montessori	Agazzi	Reggio Emilia
• Ratio—1:20/25 (1 teacher and 1 non-teaching aide). Teachers protect pupils' concentration. • Children learn best in a prepared environment. • Montessori removed typical school desks from the classroom, replacing them with tables and chairs. It also removed the teacher's desk, as the teacher should be involved with the children.	• Community of learners where the child reveals his/her inner life. • All children are seen as part of the community and make a contribution. • The exploration of the environment to find new, stimulating activities. • It is an "open" school aiming at full education; it is open to the real child and to the social and family context within which he/she lives his/her life. • The child is someone around whom we should arrange and organize an educational environment in which he/she can express himself/herself and grow.	• Environment should be welcoming to the children. • Environment should be pleasant. • Short period of time in the classroom. • Different languages are welcome.

Table 5.3. Teaching

Montessori	Agazzi	Reggio Emilia
• Teachers are trained to teach one child at a time and to oversee 20 or more children working on a broad array of tasks. • Teachers make children the center of learning. • Encourage children to learn by providing freedom within prepared environment. • Observe children to prepare the best possible environment.	• "To prepare—the educational environment" (Rosa Agazzi). • Teachers direct educational activities to "grow the child as a whole: good, thoughtful, practical, polite, useful to himself/herself and to others" (Rosa Agazzi). • "Culture" and "consciousness" are fundamental attitudes that can still characterize the professional identity of teachers in the nursery school. • spontaneous drawing • singing • drama • easy, small jobs with stuff that children like to collect (shells, pebbles, buttons).	• The teacher and other adults learn from the children. • Inquiry-based learning. • Teachers in Reggio learning environments always observe and respond to what children are doing.

Table 5.4. Learning Objectives and Activities

Montessori	Agazzi	Reggio Emilia
Three basic areas of child involvement: • Practical life or motor education. • Sensory materials—purpose is to train children's senses to focus on some obvious, particular quality, and to sharpen children's power of observation. • Academic materials—writing before reading; integrating reading and writing, and mathematics.	• Playing is a resource for learning and establishing new relationships. • The Agazzi school offers activities that stimulate communication, visual, musical, dramatic, mass-media, and multimedia expressions. • "To make" becomes an essential part of the experience of the self, in order to get expertise, independence and to develop an individual identity. • The acquisition of symbolic languages that enable the child to know how to read and decode.	• Children are at the center of the educational process. • Children learn by using all their senses. • Parents are expected to collaborate. • Teachers and parents work collaboratively. • Arts is an essential component. • Documentation is an important part.

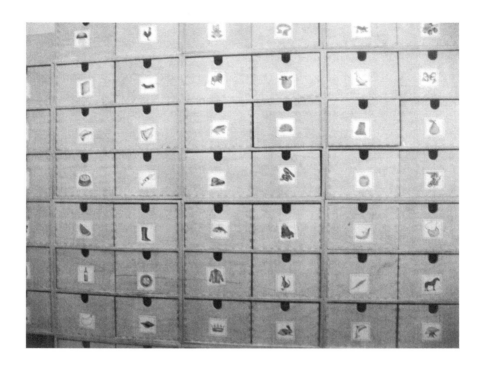

Each child's picture was also displayed on a chart on the wall, allowing each child to take his or her own attendance, and each picture was coupled with a symbol representing a task that was assigned to the child ahead of time. The children wore their own aprons displaying their symbols. Days of the week were also taught in a unique way. As the number of days increased in a week, it coincided with the increase in the number of activities per day.

Each corner in the classroom had a space where the children could engage in an activity, whether it was a reading corner, a meeting corner, or a dramatic play area. The workshop room was set up so that materials could be easily accessed by the children. Drawers with symbols on them carried ribbons, Styrofoam, buttons, and various other arts and crafts materials. The tables in the room were wooden and colorful, and were washable and laminated. The children were also each assigned a drawer where they could store the items they gathered. The teacher would regularly check each drawer to ensure the children were keeping things in order. In this way, the children learned to take care of their own things. The children were treated as protectors of their school, so they took charge of organizing their environment.

The school also believed in the importance of family involvement. The teachers welcomed family members when the children arrived at school. Upon arriving at the school, the children removed their street shoes and put on school shoes. They then stored their belongings in their cubicles and began free play. At the beginning of the day, the teacher gathered the children in a circle, planned the activities of the day, and assigned jobs to each child. At times, the children were grouped homogenously by age; at other times, the three-, four-, and five-year-old children were placed together.

The children wore aprons and caps to do their daily jobs. During gardening activities, the teachers wanted the children to experience planting and having direct contact with the soil, but some of the parents did not want the children to get dirty, so the teachers let them wear gloves to help with the planting. Parents played an active role in the day-to-day activities and were able to voice their opinion in any given situation. Together, the children and the teachers planted seeds during the winter. They also had an animal farm and bird sanctuary in the school backyard. The children harvested corn and fed the animals on the school farm. During lunch, each

child had a job to set up the table; distribute ceramic plates, cups, and glass utensils; bring in food items; or clean up afterward. The teachers would join the children for a three-course lunch, and the children would act as waiters, wearing chefs' hats.

The Teaching Concept

The director of the school mentioned that in order for a child to learn, the learning must take place in the child's natural environment. For children, the natural environment would be the home environment, which the school reproduces. Another theory is that it is important to start teaching children things they are interested in. To find out what a child would like to learn about, one can look in their pockets, as children usually keep items of interest in their pockets. Children learn by looking at real-life objects; for example, they can learn color from looking at an apple, or shapes by playing with a ball. As a result, the children are able to make better connections, and learning becomes natural instead of forced. Children learn by doing and through social interactions with each other.

Discussion and Conclusion

The environment seemed very welcoming for the children, as it was bright, cheerful, and very homey. The prevalence of symbols helped children identify their items and gave them a sense of belonging. Art was prevalent everywhere in the classroom, and children spent a great deal of time exploring different materials in the art room. The children were happy and working independently, with little adult intervention, though the teachers were available whenever the children needed help.

Similar to the Reggio Emilia approach, in this classroom the environment was the third teacher (Strong-Wilson & Ellis, 2007). In this Agazzi school, the environment helped the children feel independent enough to work by themselves. The teachers were very warm and loving toward the children, and were always smiling. It seemed that both the children and the teachers were happy to be there. The parents trusted the teachers and had a good relationship with them. The aspect we particularly appreciated was the documentation book—a huge photo album that was created by the teachers, containing the daily activities in which the children took part. The parents were shown these documents from time to time in order for them to see their child's progress and therefore feel a sense of pride.

SUMMARY

- Play is an important learning tool for children. Play encourages abstract thought, allows learning to be augmented by competent peers, and encourages self-talk.
- Play is a source of pleasure and self-expression.
- Play is beneficial to children in a number of ways. For example, it contributes to a better quality of life, represents a form of therapy, promotes intellectual development, teaches the frames and scripts of social life, enhances language development as well as interpersonal communication and social development, encourages self-regulation, and gives children the opportunity to expend extra energy.
- The project approach can be defined as in-depth investigation of a subject that is meaningful for children. It consists of three phases: (1) Introduction phase of project (2) Investigation phase, and (3) Documentation phase.

Thinking Questions

1. What are some of the effective practices to benefit children in their learning process?
2. In your opinion, what constitutes a conducive learning environment in a natural setting for the best interest of children?
3. Discuss the strength and limitations of an open learning environment as compared to the traditional school setting for children's education.

REFERENCES

Aslan, D., & Köksal Akyol, A. (2006). Okul öncesi eğitimde proje yaklaşımı. *Mesleki Eğitim Dergisi, 8*(16),87–105. (In Turkish).

Beneke, S. (2003). Strategies to incorporate literacy in project work in the pre-kindergarten classroom. In J. E. Helm (Ed.), *The project approach catalog 4: Literacy and project work*. Urbana, IL: Early Childhood and Parenting Collaborative, University of Illinois.

Biçakçi, M. Y., & Gürsoy, F. (2010). A study on the effects of project based education on the developmental areas of children. *International Journal of Academic Research, 2*(5). Retrieved from http://web.ebscohost.com.jerome.stjohns.edu:81/ehost/pdfviewer/pdfviewer?vid=3&hid=112&sid=d09c8e07-f157-4eff-b80f-9fb7ced0afc8%40sessionmgr112.

Bredekamp, S. (1987). *Developmentally appropriate practice in early childhood programs serving children from birth through age 8*. Washington, DC: National Association for the Education of Young Children

Bruner, J. (1983). Play, thought and language. *Peabody Journal of Education, 60* (3), 60–69.

Bullard, J. (2013) *Creating environments for learning: Birth to age eight. 2nd Edition*. Upper Saddle River, NJ: Merrill Pearson.

Bullard, J., & Hitz, R. (1997). Early childhood education and adult education: Bridging the cultures. *Journal of Early Childhood Teacher Education, 18*(1), 15–22.

Cadwell, L. (2003). *Bringing learning to life: The Reggio approach to early childhood education*. New York: Teachers College Press.

Chard, S.C. (2000). The challenges and the rewards: A study of teachers undertaking their first projects. Retrieved from http.//ericeece.org/pubs/book/katzsym/chard.pdf. Erişim tarihi:09.09.2008.

Chard, S.C. (2003). The project approach in action. In J. H. Helm (Ed.) *The project approach catalog 4: Literacy and project work* (2–3). Urbana, IL: Early Childhood and Parenting Collaborative, University of Illinois.

Cosco, N., & Moore, R. (1999). Playing in place: Why the physical environment is important in playwork. Presented at 14th Playeducation Annual Play and Human Development Meeting, Theoretical Playwork, Ely, Cambridgeshire, UK.

Currie, L. C. (2001). A project approach to language learning: Linking literary genres and themes. *Resource Links, Proquest Education Journals*, 6(4), 38.

Curtis, D. (2002). The power of projects. *Educational Leadership*, 6(1), 50–53.

DeGennaro, A. K. (2012). Young investigators: The project approach in the early years, 2nd Edition. *Journal of Experiental Education, 35* (1), 305–306.

Dungi, D., Sebest, H., Thompson, A., & Young, L. (2002). The apple project. *Early Childhood Research and Practice*, 4(2), 75–93.

Durlak, J. A., Mahoney, J. L., Bohnert, A. M., & Parente, M. E. (2010, June). Developing and improving after-school programs to enhance youth's personal growth and adjustment: A special issue of AJCP. *American Journal of Community Psychology*. Pp. 285–293.

Elkind, D. (1988) *The hurried child: Growing up too fast too soon* (3rd ed.). New York: Perseus Books Group.

Elkonin, D. (1977). Toward the problem of stages in the mental development of the child. In M. Cole (Ed.), *Soviet Development Psychology*. White Plains, NY: M.E. Sharpe. (Original work published in 1971)

Elkonin, D. B. (1978). *Psychologija igry [The psychology of play]*. Moscow: Pedagogika.

Erikson, E. H. (1963). *Childhood and society* (2nd ed.). New York: Norton.

Freud, S. (1915). *The Unconscious. Standard Edition*, 14: 159–204.

Froebel, F. (1912). Froebel's chief writings on education. Retrieved from http://core.roehampton.ac.uk/digital/froarc/frochi

Gutek, G. L. (Ed.). (2004). *The Montessori method: The origins of an educational innovation: Including an abridged and annotated edition of Maria Montessori's the Montessori method*. Lanham, MD: Rowman & Littlefield.

Helm, J. H. (2004). Projects that power young minds. *Educational Leadership*, 62(1), 58–62.

Helm, J. H., & Katz, G. L. (2001). *Young investigator: The project approach in the early years*. New York and London: Teacher Collage Press.

Hewett, V. M. (2001). Examining the Reggio Emilia approach to early childhood education. *Early Childhood Education Journal*, 29(2), 95–100.

Ho, R. (2001). Implementing project approach in Hong Kong preschool. Retrieved from http://eric.ed.gov.

Johnson, J. E., Christie, J. F., & Wardle, F. (2005). *Play, development and early education*. Upper Saddle River, NJ: Merrill/Pearson.

Johnson, L. V. (2005). A fair play unit for elementary school: Getting the whole school involved. *Teaching Elementary Physical Education, 16*(3), 16–19.

Katz, G. L., & Chard, S. C. (2000). *Engaging children's minds: the project approach*. Stamford, CT: Ablex Publishing Corporation.

Katz, G. L., & Chard, S. C. (2000). The Project Approach: An Overview. In J. L. Roopnarine & J. E. Johnson (Eds.) *Approaches to Early Childhood Education*. Columbus, OH: Merrill Publication.

Kim, H., Park, E., & Lee, J. (2001). All done! Take it home. Then into a trash-can?: displaying and using children's art projects. *Early Childhood Education, 29*(1), 41–50.

Kucharski, G. A., Rust, J. O., & Ring, T. R. (Summer 2005). Evaluation of the ecological futures and global (EFG) curriculum: A project based approach. *Education, 125*(4), 652–668.

Laminack, L. L., & Lawing, S. (1994). Building curriculum. *Primary Voices, 6*.

LeeKeenan, D., & Edwards, C. P. (1992). Using the project approach with tod-dlers. *Young Children, 47*(4), 31–35.

Lichtenberg, P., & Norton, D. G. (1972). *Cognitive and mental development in the first five years of life;: A review of recent research*. National Institute of Mental Health.

Liebovich, B. J. (2000). Children's self-assessment. Retrieved from http://ericeece.org/pubs/books/katzsym/liebovich.pdf.

MacDonell, C. (2007). Signs all around us: A project approach unit for kinder-garten. *Library Media Connection*, 32–34.

Malaguzzi, L. (1998). History, ideas, and basic philosophy: An interview with Lella Gandini. In C. Edwards, L. Gandini, & G. Forman (Eds.), *The hundred languages of children: The Reggio Emilia approach—advanced reflections* (2nd ed.) (49–98). Greenwich, CT: Ablex.

Montessori, M. (1989). *Education for a new world*. Oxford, UK: Clio. (Original work published in 1946)

Myler, T. (2003). Why does snow get dirty? My first experience with the project approach. In J.H. Helm (Ed.) *The project approach catalog 4: Literacy and Project work* (2–5). Urbana, IL: Early Childhood and Parenting Collaborative, University of Illinois.

New, R. S. (1993) Reggio Emilia: Some lessons for U.S. educators. *ERIC Digests*, ED354988.

Parten, M. B. (1932). Social participation among preschool children. *The Journal of Abnormal and Social Psychology, 27*, 243–269.

Piaget, J. (1947/62). *Play, dreams, and imitation in early childhood.* London: Routledge.

Plekhanov, A. (1992). The pedagogical theory and practice of Maria Montessori. *Russian Education and Society, 34*(3), 83–96.

Riley, D., San Juan, R. R., Klinker, J., & Ramminger, A. (2008). *Social & emotional development: Connecting science and practice in early childhood settings.* St. Paul, MN: Redleaf Press.

Ryser, G. R., Beeler, J. E., & McKenzie, C. M. (1995). Effects of a Computer-Supported Intentional Learning Environment (CSILE) on students' self-concept, self-regulatory behavior, and critical thinking ability. *Journal of Educational Computing Research, 13*, 375–385.

Seitz, H., & Bartholomew, C. (2008). Powerful Portfolios for Young Children. *Early Childhood Education Journal, 36*(1), 63–68.

Strong-Wilson, T., Ellis, J. (Winter 2007). Children and place: Reggio Emilia's environment as third teacher. *Theory into Practice, 46* (1), 40–47

Tuğrul, B. (2002). Properties of project approach. *Journal of Child Development and Education, 1*(6/7), 71–79. (In Turkish).

Vygotsky, L. (1930). *The socialist alteration of man*, in van Der Veer, R., and Vasliner, J., Eds. (1998). *The Vygotsky Reader*, Oxford: Blackwell.

Weikart, D. P., & Schweinhart, L. J. (2000). The high/scope curriculum for early childhood care and education. Chapter 11 in J. L. Roopnarine & J. E. Johnson, *Approaches to early childhood education* (3rd ed.). Upper Saddle River, NJ: Merrill/Prentice Hall.

Chapter Six

Health, Safety, and Nutrition Education for Young Children

Recent brain research demonstrates that the physical, emotional, and intellectual development of young children depends on proper nutrition. Because it plays such an important role in promoting development, nutrition also helps children do well in school. Numerous studies have proved the link between nutrition and academic performance as measured by test scores, attendance rates, tardiness, and discipline. "Because research has confirmed a link between nutrition and children's cognitive development, cognitive performance, and ability to concentrate, preschool and school-age children need to receive proper and adequate nutrition" (ERIC Digest, 1994).

According to the Children's Defense Fund, approximately 13.6 million children suffer from malnutrition in the United States (Wardle, Herrera, Cooke, & Gibson, 2003). "Several federal nutrition education programs, including Head Start, the Nutrition Education and Training (NET) program, and the special supplemental nutrition rogram for Women, Infants, and Children (WIC), have been providing nutrition-education services to some families for many years." These numbers are startling considering that there are numerous and widespread nutrition education programs, including the Nutrition Education and Training (NET) program and food-based educational services provided by the Special Supplemental Nutrition Program for Women, Infants, and Children (WIC), to name just two (Fuhr & Barclay, 1998). These programs, along with US Department of Agriculture (USDA) supplemental food programs, attempt to curb the rise of this very serious problem by providing subsidies and food to parents and children, both in the home and through the nationwide school lunch program.

Unfortunately, some of these programs have not kept up with the most recent information regarding good nutritional habits for children. Too often, the programs provide high-fat, low-vitamin diets that do not promote health, and therefore, child development. Due to the fact that children are in school for a substantial portion of the day, the US Department of Education plays a critical role in helping teachers learn healthy eating habits. Effective school nutritional policies help children learn to make healthy choices in their selection of foods. Evidence suggests that the agency recognizes the role it plays in promoting childhood nutrition; the Department of Education, for example, recently stated that well-fed, well-nourished children are better equipped to learn. Therefore, over the next few years, this department will provide cities like New York City with more appealing and nutritious foods for schools and more inviting dining environments for teachers (New York City Department of Education, 2010).

EFFECTS OF POOR NUTRITION

As mentioned in a study by Neergaard (2006), "Far too many kids are fat by preschool, and Hispanic youngsters are most at risk, says new research that's among the first to focus on children growing up in poverty." The maintenance of a healthy weight, starting in childhood, provides a healthy pathway for students to follow, helping them avoid many of the additional health risks that are associated with obesity. Being obese increases immediate health risks for young people, including type 2 diabetes, mental health effects from low self-esteem, depression, and poor school performance. Obesity also increases risk factors for long-term cardiovascular health such as high blood pressure and cholesterol, as well as for some forms of cancer. According to the National Institutes of Health, childhood obesity has tripled since 1970. Currently, about 20 percent of US children are overweight and those who remain that way during their teenage years are highly likely to be overweight as adults (Jacobson, 2004). Thus, young children who grow up with poor nutrition or poor nutritional habits tend to perform worse academically and lead less healthy, productive, and enjoyable lives. Though New York City is taking actions to supply children with healthier lunches, kids are still selecting less nutritious food outside of school. This indicates a significant break in the school-home community model discussed earlier.

Although parents and teachers recognize the importance of their children's health and nutrition, they need to also learn how to encourage their children to select the right kinds of food. Our nation's educational system is not doing enough to promote healthy habits from a young age. "Children exposed to nutrition education programs . . . express more positive attitudes toward consumption of fruit and vegetables, and show improved ability to apply nutrition education behaviors in the classroom" (McDonald, Brun, & Esserman, 1981). Thus, teachers and parents need to be cognizant of nutrition and health matters and, whenever possible, go a step further by reaching out to educate other community members about these matters. Teachers and parents who are well informed should provide information about the value of nutritional diets, as well as ways for parents to make quick, easy, nutritional lunches with their kids. If children get involved in making nutritional food for themselves, they are more likely to select the right kinds of meals in and out of school.

Finally, children need to be aware of the health contributions of different foods, and in the process, be encouraged to adopt a balanced, healthy diet. This can be done through research projects and homework assignments, the additional benefit of which is that children learn about available resources on nutrition.

THE FAMILY-SCHOOL FOOD CONNECTION

According to recent literature, "Nutritionists, social scientists, and educators are able to demonstrate a positive correlation between proper nutrition and intellectual functioning resulting in improved learning" (Cosgrove, 1991). It is certainly true that a well-nourished child is usually an active child, and a child who is active learns more. As Cosgrove (1991) explains, "Healthy, well-nourished children benefit more from formal education than undernourished children." Therefore, children need to be educated about proper nutrition, and so do their parents. Education around food is important for families, and enables them to make good nutritional decisions (Cosgrove, 1991). During the early childhood years, when children tend to have an "absorbent mind" (Montessori, 1965), they should learn about nutrition. As Cosgrove (1991) states, "Particularly during the early years when children are both an impressionable and a captive audience, and when habits are formed, nutrition education is critical to the formation of health-promoting nutritional concepts and behaviors. It is during these early years that nutrition education is most successful."

The importance of parents practicing good food habits cannot be stressed enough; as Piaget and other child development theorists have pointed out, children imitate adults, and therefore, "adults must be mindful of the nutrient needs of children and must use this knowledge in shaping children's food preferences and patterns" (Fuhr & Barclay, 1998). Experience and studies in preschools have shown that, even in these early years, children can be led beyond the names and tastes of foods to an understanding of basic concepts of nutritive value, nutrient function, and the impact of nutrition on health (Swadener, 1995).

Name

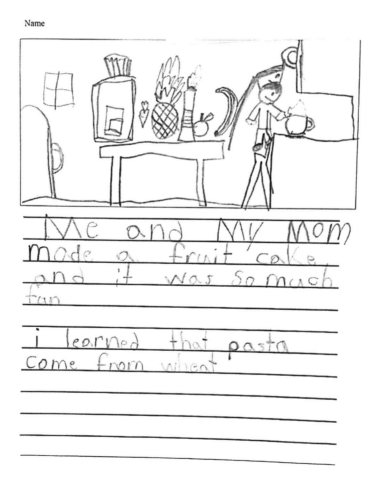

Since children spend a lot of time at school, schools should take an active role in nutrition education among children. According to the New York City Department of Education (2007), breakfast and lunch times could be instructional periods that afford teachers opportunities to structure learning environments that promote food and nutrition education, as well as social interaction, development of concepts and skills, and self-directed activities, all of which present children with choices. Often, children at an early age cannot clearly distinguish between healthy and unhealthy options. Further, teachers must factor in the influence that family has over children; Cosgrove (1991) mentions that, "Total commitment from parents is a crucial part of any nutrition program." Since its inception, for example, Head Start has emphasized the importance of respecting family food preferences and eating patterns, while providing nutrition education; from the organization's perspective, both are critical to the development of sound nutritional concepts and behaviors (Fuhr & Barclay, 1998). Furthermore, childhood obesity has rapidly increased and has become one of the most alarming public health issues. The child's home is likely to have the greatest influence on his or her eating and physical activity behaviors. "Supportive school interventions can only reinforce and complement any effort to prevent obesity that happens in the home" (Sutherland, Gill, & Binns, 2004).

As we have seen, schools play an important role in helping children and their families. Families view teachers as resources; the onus falls on teachers, then, to be resources for parents, especially in the arena of child nutrition and health.

Nutrition is an interdisciplinary topic that could very well be integrated across the curriculum in the classroom. One idea mentioned by Cosgrove (1991) involves cooking with children. By engaging students in actual nutritional activities, all of their senses become engaged by the process, opening the door to experiential learning.

ROLE OF TEACHERS IN NUTRITION EDUCATION

Since teachers are able to inspire children, they play a key role in motivating children to learn about health and nutrition. Thus, teachers should be knowledgeable about these matters, so they can better convey information to children and parents. A number of other school stakeholders, including supervisors, principals, and teacher-educators at universities, can also play important roles in this process. For example, teacher-educators should encourage young teachers to register for courses on health and nutrition instruction. The next section will focus on examples of ways to engage students in actively learning about health, wellness, and nutrition.

Courses on health and nutrition instruction will help teachers to be aware of the resources they can use to effectively teach the children. Nutrition information can be imparted to children in a variety of ways. In the following project, using the food pyramid as a guide, teachers developed a nutrition file and a nutrition bag. The purpose of the nutrition file was to encourage teachers to gather resources as future teaching materials. The objective of the nutrition bag was to provide materials to the parents in order to establish an effective school-to-home connection.

THE NUTRITION PROJECT

The project consists of three parts. In the first part of the assignment, teachers, either individually or as a team, gather resources and teaching ideas from books, journals, and the Internet on health and nutrition, taking advantage of the wealth of resources that already exists on both of these subjects. This can be a cooperative group project for the teachers, perhaps for teams of teachers working in the same school. Each group contains five teachers, and each teacher is assigned one of the five food groups: bread/grains, fruits, vegetables, meat/proteins, and dairy products. The teachers then select a few resources that focus on the needs of their children. The teachers then turn rudimentary teaching ideas into concrete lesson plans that integrate different curricular areas and put those in a nutrition file. The second part of the project is to administer lesson plans and teach children. The third part involves creating nutrition bags for parents to take home and to review with their children; they contain additional resources on health and nutrition, such as activities, games, songs, books, cooking recipes, and plans for visits to grocery stores, bakeries, restaurants, and other food establishments. The bags also contain letters that summarize these resources for parents, as well as short surveys that parents are asked to fill out, evaluating the impact of the nutrition project. Finally, teachers hand in written reflections on the nutrition project.

Information on this project will be provided from four teachers: two are regular classroom teachers from public schools in New York, while the other two are volunteer teachers from private schools in New York. The sample is from Queens, New York, and all of the children included in the study were three to seven years old. In the study, teachers were required to make nutrition files and nutrition bags. With the instructor's help, every teacher had at least a small group of students to implement the project. Each teacher also distributed nutrition bags to two to five parents.

Overall Objectives of the Nutrition Project:

1. Assess the kinds of foods children typically eat.
2. Using the food pyramid, teach children about the five food groups and the variety of foods within each group.
3. Expose children to a variety of foods and ways of preparing different foods.
4. Teach children about healthy and unhealthy foods and how to make healthy choices.
5. Evaluate children's capacities to select healthy foods and help them gain a general understanding of the importance of a healthy diet.

Project Design:

Pre-test. All the children were given a pre-test to evaluate the extent to which they could select healthy foods. The questionnaire was pictorial and included questions with a few choices that the children had to circle.

Instruction. Teachers introduced the unit to the whole class, presented the food pyramid, read a book about health and nutrition, and sang songs about health with the children. Teachers then divided the children into smaller groups, each of which completed a different game. Every game was designed to engage a different skill or subject, while simultaneously teaching the children about health; for example, the games involved math, science, language arts, social studies, and music. After a group completed one game, it would move on to another game; the groups completed each game in a rotation. Then, at the closing circle, teachers reinforced lessons learned from the topic of the day.

Post-test. The children participating in the study were given a post-test to evaluate their capacity to select healthy foods. Teachers administered a pictorial questionnaire similar to the one given previously to children, and asked them to circle their answers. Teachers also asked the children informal questions to gauge how much they'd learned from the project, and if they'd enjoyed the activities.

To further the home-school connection, teachers also sent nutrition bags home. The bags consisted of letters informing parents about the project, along with games, activities, books, puzzles, jokes, riddles, and ideas for trips to the grocery store. Finally, the bags also had surveys for parents to complete, which would give teachers some information about how much children had learned from the project.

Findings: Teacher 1

In the report, Teacher 1 mentioned, "Nutrition is a very important topic that should be incorporated in the early childhood science curriculum. Nutrition teaches young children how to take care of themselves in different ways. It revolves around the theme of being healthy by keeping fit, eating healthy food, and practicing good hygiene. It is paramount that young children should be taught to practice these good habits early on so that they can continue to use them throughout their lives."

The overall objectives for this teacher were to teach her kindergarten students about making healthier food choices on an everyday basis and becoming familiar with the food groups. She witnessed that "many of my past and present students bring their own snacks and lunches to school and [I] was not surprised to find their lunchboxes filled with potato chips, candies, and chocolates." Therefore, she wanted to use this project to make her students more knowledgeable about nutrition and more capable of making healthy food choices for themselves. She also wanted to teach them about the Food Guide Pyramid and how it can be used to identify which foods they should eat more of, and which ones they should eat in moderation.

The teacher gathered her students in the circle time area and explained the difference between everyday food and "once in a while" food. They understood this concept right away and even began to identify "once in a while" foods that they were familiar with, such as potato chips, candy, gum, and soda. For example, a student named Oli (all names are pseudonyms) stated, "I know some foods that I should only eat once in a while such as M&Ms and cotton candy. I can't eat cotton candy all the time because it has a lot of sugar and mommy said that my teeth will fall out if I eat too much candy." Sarah supported this statement by saying, "Yeah, a lot of candy is not good for my body. If I eat a lot of candy and drink a lot of soda, my body will be full of junk food and then I won't grow." The teacher then presented her students with picture cards displaying different foods, including potato chips, an apple, a lollipop, a doughnut, broccoli, soda, milk, a cheese sandwich, gum, chocolate chip cookies, a baked chicken, and a banana. As a group, the children identified each food. She then wrote two columns on the chalkboard, with one column titled "Everyday Foods" and the other titled "Once in a while Foods." As she held up each picture card, the teacher called on volunteers to identify which category the foods fell in, and had them tape up the picture cards in the appropriate columns. To her surprise, the students labeled each picture correctly. Together, the teacher and her students reviewed the results and came to a unanimous agreement about how to categorize each pictured food. Under the "Everyday Foods" column, they attached pictures of the apple, broccoli, milk, cheese sandwich, baked chicken, and banana. Under the "Once in a while Foods" column, they taped up the potato chips, lollipop, doughnut, soda, gum, and chocolate chip cookies.

After this activity, the teacher presented her students with a large poster of the Food Guide Pyramid. She first asked them what they thought the poster was trying to convey. Some of their responses included: "That's a cool pyramid. I think it tells us about different food." Another child mentioned, "I think the pyramid is about the foods we eat like chicken, bread, cheese, and carrots." One student named Tom said, "I think the pyramid is about making different foods, like how my mom can make bread and cook meat at home." The teacher then asked them to notice the shape of the pyramid, particularly how the top of the pyramid was smaller than the bottom. The teacher mentioned that she initially thought that none of her students would understand the meaning behind this but was surprised when one child raised his hand and said, "The foods on the top of the pyramid are the foods that we should not eat a lot of, such as the candies, because that space is small so that means we should not eat a lot of those foods. When the space gets bigger like when the pyramid goes down, it means we eat more of those foods, because those are the foods that make us healthier so we should eat a lot of grapes, corn, and bread." The teacher was very pleased with this statement because the student displayed logical thinking skills and the other children understood his explanation.

The teacher then read out the parts of the pyramid for her class. Students learned that the Food Guide Pyramid is divided into six food groups: fats, oils, and sweets; milk, yogurt, and cheese; meat, poultry, fish, dry beans, eggs, and nuts; vegetables; fruits; and breads, cereals, rice, and pasta. She then hung up another poster of the Food Guide Pyramid but this time, the poster did not contain any pictures. She taped this blank Food Guide Pyramid poster next to the illustrated poster and presented pictures of different foods. She asked the class to identify which group each food belonged to and instructed them to tape pictures in the correct sections of the blank Food Guide Pyramid. Using the illustrated Food Guide Pyramid as a guide, all of the volunteers successfully placed each pictured food in the correct food group. They ended this activity by reviewing everyday healthy and once in a while food choices, as well as the six food groups on the Food Guide Pyramid. The students also learned that they should have more servings of bread, cereal, rice, and pasta than other types of food. Finally, the teacher concluded the activity with the "Making Bread" song, the lyrics for which were posted on chart paper for the entire class to see. As the students sang the song, she pointed to the words on the chart paper. They excitedly repeated the song three times.

From this pre-test measurement, the teacher learned that her students were able to identify healthy and non-healthy foods. They also used language to explain their understanding of healthy food choices. This was the first time the students were introduced to the Food Guide Pyramid, but they had little difficulty understanding the basic food groups. They also gained new knowledge of the food groups and were better able to identify the foods that belong to each group.

In the next part of the lesson, the children were divided into three small groups—the Breads and Grains Group (four children), the Vegetable Group (four children), and the Fruit Group (five children). The teacher placed the Breads and Grains Group in the kitchen area and gave them yellow and brown play dough. She told them that they were all "chefs" and that their job was to make as much bread, cereal, rice, and pasta as they could with the play dough.

For the Vegetable Group and Fruit Group, the teacher created two separate "supermarkets" in the dramatic play area. Each supermarket had a variety of plastic foods. The job of each group was for students to work cooperatively with each other and shop for either vegetables (Vegetable Group) or fruits (Fruit Group). Once each group received their items, each group was instructed to bring their "groceries" back to a designated table and make a list of the vegetables or fruits they had bought by taking turns drawing them on chart paper.

The teacher walked around the classroom as the three groups were busy doing their "jobs." She observed, listened, and recorded their interactions and discussions with each other. She also noted if each group was able to stay on task. The results of the small group activities were excellent. She was very impressed with her Breads and Grains Group—they used their creativity and imagination to make a wide array of breads, pastas, rice, and cereals. As they stated, "We made spaghetti, bread slices, macaroni and cheese, yellow rice, Cheerios cereal, bagels, and muffins." Thus, the children were able to identify foods that belonged to the breads and grains food group and successfully used play dough to demonstrate their knowledge.

The Vegetable Group successfully "bought" all the vegetables from the play supermarket and the members were able to draw carrots, cucumbers, corn, potatoes, lettuce, and broccoli on the "vegetables" chart paper. The Fruit Group was also successful in "buying" fruits and drew apples, grapes, oranges, strawberries, and bananas on their "fruits" chart paper. When all of the groups were finished, the teacher had the children walk around the room, looking at and discussing each other's creations. Some of the responses were: "Wow! Look at the different breads and stuff they made. My favorite is the macaroni and cheese" (Jod); "The Breads and Grains Group did a good job. They made so much food with the play dough" (Ali); "I like how the Vegetables Group drew the broccoli. It looks like a little tree" (Myl); and "Now the Fruit Group can make fruit salad since they drew all those fruits" (Pat).

The students really enjoyed this small group activity. They were able to "play" together while learning more about food groups. They also gained hands-on experiences with real-world situations, such as shopping in the supermarket and preparing meals for themselves. The small group activity also reinforced the importance of choosing healthy food for the class. Finally, the teacher gained something from this experience, as well; she noted that, "The small group activity also reinforced my understanding as a teacher of how important it is to provide young children with center-based activities such as dramatic play. They learned so much through play and interactions with each other."

The next day, the class had an exciting discussion about what they had done the previous day, and displayed considerable enthusiasm for what they'd learned about the food groups. After a short discussion, the teacher gave the students a workbook titled "Going Shopping," which they had to complete individually. It was a "make your own book" about shopping for healthy foods, and contained eight pages (including the cover). Each page displayed a picture of a food item for children to color in, as well as a "fill in the missing letter sentence" on the top of the page. For example, on page one of the workbook, there was a picture of an apple with a sentence that read: "We need app_es." Students had to figure out the missing letter in the word *apple* and write it in. As students completed the book, the teacher walked around the classroom, observing each child's progress and guiding those who needed help. After everyone had completed the assignment, the teacher ended the "book experience" by reading aloud from *Today Is Monday* by Eric Carle. Carle's book outlines the various foods that can be eaten on each day of the week, including string beans, spaghetti, roast beef, fish, chicken, and ice cream. The book served the important purpose of reinforcing what students had learned in the previous day's activities.

Using her students' completed "Going Shopping" books, the teacher assessed each child's understanding of the unit, as well as their letter and sound recognition skills. Ten out of the thirteen students used the correct colors to depict the foods and wrote in the correct letters. The teacher also used this "make your own book" assignment as an individual activity. The students loved the reproducible books, because they had the opportunity to add personal touches to the books and make them their own. Some of the children commented: "Look at my book, I did it all by myself." The "Going Shopping" book was no different. When Oli finished her book, she came up to the teacher and said, "Look at my 'Going Shopping' book. I colored the pictures and finished the sentences with no help from anybody. I guess that makes me the author and illustrator of this book. That's cool!" The teacher was also able to teach her class about authors, illustrators, and parts of a book, reinforcing knowledge they had learned in previous lessons. The teacher stated, "When I see how proud my kindergarten students are of their work, it makes me realize that young children have the full potential to learn good work values, especially when I give them a sense of ownership in their educational experiences."

After the book activity, the teacher ended the nutrition lesson with a special snack time. Instead of the usual cookies, crackers, and pretzels, the teacher provided the class with real fruits. She gave a small fruit salad comprised of grapes, apples, bananas, and oranges to each child in a plastic cup, checking beforehand for allergies. The teacher also had a bag of potato chips. As the teacher called each child to get his or her special snack, she gave the child a choice—either potato chips or the fruit salad. The best part of this snack time was the fact that ALL of the students chose the fruit salad over the potato chips, exactly the outcome the teacher had hoped for!

Throughout the entire nutrition project, the introduction phase was the only time that the teacher felt she had to really provide additional help to her students, despite the fact that the majority of them had never been exposed to the Food Guide Pyramid and the food groups before.

The students' reactions, overall, to this project were very good. They showed interest in the topics of healthy food choices and the Food Guide Pyramid and were openly excited and enthusiastic during small group activities. They also displayed a sense of value and pride in their "Going Shopping" books during the individual activity. The teacher was happy that the project went smoothly and that the students learned about these topics in a fun and age-appropriate way. After the special snack time, Pat actually came up to the teacher and said, "The food pyramid stuff is fun. Can we do it again tomorrow?" Commenting on this, the teacher said, "It was such a fulfilling statement to hear and motivated me to plan more nutrition activities even after this project is over." Due to time constraints the teacher could not do all the food groups with the students; however, she felt that if she had had more time, she would have continued the nutrition unit beyond the planned assignments.

Nutrition Bag

In terms of the nutrition bag, the teachers prepared five bags for five food groups. Each bag contained a parent binder, full of information about nutrition and the food groups, as well as directions for using the items in the bag. The bag included activity worksheets, children's books, songs, children's games, and a parent survey. For the grains bag, the teacher included items such as a muffin tray, one blueberry muffin mix, and two packets of Quaker Instant Oatmeal.

For the assignment, the teacher distributed nutrition bags to three of the students and their parents and received three parent surveys back. The parents kept the bags over the weekend. The teacher planned to rotate bags among parents, so that each household had the chance to explore the bags' contents over a weekend.

The teacher then had individual discussions with the first three students who had already experienced the nutrition bag at home with their parents. Overall, all three thought the bag was "so much fun." Sim told the teacher, "The bag was awesome! I even helped my mom make blueberry muffins. That was the best part!" Ali said, "I liked the books. My mommy and daddy read me the books at nighttime and my dad played the memory game with me." Ju shared, "I liked the bag a lot. My mommy and daddy liked it, too, and we played the games together and read the books. My mommy made me the strawberry oatmeal for breakfast and it was so yummy!"

Based on parent surveys, the teacher felt that the nutrition bag project was very effective. The three surveys indicated that parents had very satisfying experiences with the bag, because all three gave it a very high rating (all circled "Strongly Agree" for each question evaluating the bag's effectiveness). Their comments were also uniformly positive. Sim's mother wrote, "We loved the bag—great books, games, and recipe. The binder also contained a lot of useful information for myself and all directions were so clear. I was very pleased with this home project." Ali's father wrote, "This bag was excellent. We had so much fun doing all the activities together as a family." Ju's mother commented, "The bag had so many fun and interesting things in it. Thank you for having us involved with Ju's learning about healthy foods!"

Reflecting on these statements, the teacher said, "These comments made us realize how important it is to always establish some form of parental involvement and communication. I think this part of the project with the nutrition bag was an excellent idea because I was able to establish a school-home connection. It allowed the parents and their children to enjoy quality time together while providing the children with fun and age-appropriate activities. It also made the parents feel important in their children's learning experiences."

Reflection on the Project

The teacher felt that her students learned a great deal from the project. Though they were already familiar with healthy and non-healthy foods, this project reinforced the link between making healthy food choices for them. The teacher felt her children understood this concept when, without hesitation, they all chose the fruit salad over potato chips during the special snack time. When teachers and parents take the time to educate and guide young children on how to eat better, children are more likely to adopt better eating habits and to monitor their own food choices on an everyday basis.

The students also gained new knowledge about the Food Guide Pyramid and its six food groups. Furthermore, they learned which food groups they should have more servings of and which ones they should eat in limited quantities. It was especially helpful for them to construct their own pyramids. Finally, the activity strengthened their capacity to work cooperatively together in small groups and gave them a feeling of accomplishment and pride in their work.

Educating parents about this topic and having them involved in their children's learning experiences are also vital forces that encourage children to eat healthier. The nutrition bag is a great strategy to get the parents involved and to establish healthier eating habits at home. It also creates school-home communication and a sense of teamwork between parents and teacher.

As for myself, I gained new appreciation for this topic on nutrition and my role as an early childhood teacher. This project made me sit back and realize that what I do as a teacher is very important. Not only do I teach my young students their basic reading and writing skills, but I also have the responsibility to teach them how to take care of themselves physically and how to be well-rounded individuals. Along with new teaching strategies, this nutrition project also taught me the importance of being an effective teacher and truly caring about my students' health.

Findings: Teacher 2

As part of the second-grade science curriculum, and as a continuation of the body organs and health unit, the teacher devoted the last few days to teaching children about the food groups. They read the book *What Happens to a Hamburger?* by Paul Showers, and students created individual nutrition books by cutting and pasting food items from magazines in a collage depicting breakfast, lunch, and dinner. The teacher commented on this activity, "When I was working on the nutrition project and the nutrition file (for my assignment), I realized how much quality information was actually missing from the lesson. In a way, doing this report, I had the opportunity to reopen the lesson using the selected items from the file in order to build not only the students' interests but also [those] of the parents toward this very important topic." She decided to divide the lesson over a period of three days so that the individual activities would not overlap and all the children would be able to participate in every project. In one PTA meeting, the teacher had the opportunity to speak with parents about her plans for reopening the health unit. She outlined her intention to place five students in a class of twenty-six into each of the five food groups, with the remaining student joining the grains group. Each group was placed at their own table, and each knew what their table represented. At the PTA meeting, the teacher asked parents to supply the class with utensils, food items, empty food cartons, cans, juice containers, and more. The teacher also requested three parents to volunteer during the cooking session, which took place on the final day of the lesson. The teacher has a good rapport with the parents, and thus was able to explain the importance of teaching proper nutrition to children when they are young. Parents were extremely excited about the project and that their children would learn about an important topic in school.

Objectives

The objectives of the lesson were for students to be able to classify different foods into the correct categories of the Food Guide Pyramid, to identify foods that keep our bodies healthy, and to learn to look for foods from each food group when they visit the supermarket.

Initially, the teacher displayed the overhead picture of the pyramid and said, "Today we are going to learn about the Food Guide Pyramid and what all the colors mean." She explained that the Food Guide Pyramid has been changed since the last time they looked at it, and had the students identify the new changes. Because the students had already been exposed to the topic, the teacher refreshed their memories by asking questions like: "Why do you think you need to eat?" and "What kinds of food do you think are nutritious and good for you?" She then discussed students' ideas about nutrition. Pointing to the Food Guide Pyramid chart, she asked the children if they had any questions regarding its design. One frequent question asked was, "Why do people choose a pyramid instead of any other solid shape?" Instead of giving the class a ready answer, the teacher asked the children to draw any other shape on a piece of paper, divide it into six parts, and narrow the top of each part until it looked like a pointy tip. The teacher observed that the children struggled to do this, and then she asked, "Is that possible?" The children shouted in relief, "No way!" So the students were able to figure out why the pyramid was the perfect solid shape to show the narrowing of each food group. One child expressed her confusion about the colors of the dairy and protein groups. Another child answered her classmate's question, "Milk is white and it won't look pretty in a white paper, so that's why they picked blue." A third student, Yan, added, "Maybe people just voted for their favorite color."

In the next part of the activity, the teacher asked students to look at their individual food pyramids, lists of foods in each group, and also a sheet explaining the serving portions. She explained clearly on the board what one serving means; an ounce equals one piece of bread, a half cup of cooked cereal, or a half cup of rice or pasta. The children were able to recognize fractions, which they had just finished reviewing the week before. She then asked the students to discuss what kinds of food they were eating every day. Students suggested meals and then identified the food groups and number of servings included in their suggestions. Students' favorite dishes were spaghetti and pizza; the teacher asked which food groups these items belong in. To give an example, the teacher showed what she ate that day; interestingly, the class was not only able to figure out how to categorize what she'd eaten, but was also quick to point out that she'd consumed an excessive amount of grains. For homework, students were given the "My Pyramid Worksheet" to be filled out at home, which asked them to list what they ate yesterday, what they had already eaten today, and then create a plan for what to eat tomorrow.

On the second day, the teacher began the lesson by asking students to read their completed worksheets aloud, and the class then discussed the different ways people eat their meals. Maya mentioned that her family is vegetarian. This led the conversation in a whole new direction; the students learned that people can enjoy eating beans and get enough protein from a vegetarian diet without eating any meat. The teacher also presented the food counter display, which she had arranged early in the morning by gathering food containers from various food groups, such as cereal boxes, juice, food labels, and ingredients lists from bread, candy, chocolates, cookie boxes, cans, and soda bottles. This display literally made the counter into a mini-store for students to explore. The teacher asked the class to take a stroll around the mock store and read container labels. After fifteen minutes, they gathered to discuss their observations. Almost all of the children could figure out that the foods represented were high in sugar. Finally, the teacher handed out crossword puzzles and worksheets to each student, reviewing what the assignment required. She pointed out the words "whole grain" on the ingredient label and then asked students if they had seen this phrase on the classroom display shelf.

Later the teacher asked students to name vegetables they had seen or eaten and talk about their favorite fruits. She also asked them to name some items in the milk group. Sahel said, "I get sick when I drink milk!" Three other children agreed with him. This led to further discussion about lactose intolerance and the availability of lactose-free products. Afterward, the teacher asked the class to name foods from the meat and beans group. After the discussion, she asked the students to choose two books from the shelf to read for the read-aloud session. Amy picked *Stone Soup* and Lan chose *Everybody Cooks Rice*. Each student took a turn doing oral reading, and then the teacher asked the students a few critical thinking questions to assess their knowledge of the contents of each book. For the last twenty-five minutes of class, the teacher divided the laminated food cards among the five teams and each team received "Pyramid Go Fish" instructions, which she read to them step by step, demonstrating the rules to team leaders in a mock game. Then team leaders were charged with the task of teaching the game to the group. For the next twenty-five minutes, the class was filled with laughter and loud conversations as the groups played the game.

On the third and final day of the unit, the teacher planned an event, something that everyone was really looking forward to: the cooking project! The entire school got to know about it. The teacher used three hours for the project, and three parent volunteers and the teacher set up tables in the lunchroom. They had two blenders, one big pot, three small kitchen knives (for parents to handle), measuring spoons, cups, plastic knives, mixing spoons, cutting boards, serving plates, mixing bowls, plastic glasses, one rice cooker, a small electric stove, and one can opener. There was a chart paper showing the rules for handling food. The children washed their hands, wore aprons, and put on clear plastic gloves. The food items were placed on each table corresponding to the food groups. For the grains table, there was a rice cooker, two cups of rice, water, one loaf of whole wheat bread, one large plate for holding the vegetables that would be supplied by the vegetable group, one bottle of mustard, one bottle of ketchup, one cutting board, and plastic knives. For the dairy table, there was one blender, measuring cups, measuring spoons, a half gallon of low-fat milk, one quart of lactose-free milk, Mott's Applesauce, cinnamon powder, and sugar in a zip-lock bag. For the protein table, there was one container of yogurt, four seven-ounce cans of tuna, black pepper, mint leaves, canned French beans, red kidney beans, chickpeas, sugar in a zip-lock bag, one small bottle of olive oil, and vinegar. Also for the protein table there was deli-sliced turkey (one pound), deli-sliced cheese (one pound), one packet of salt, one big bowl, one big spoon, serving spoons, and plates. For the fruit table, there were bananas, frozen peaches, strawberries, one gallon of apple juice, one blender, plastic cups, and one cutting board. For the vegetable table, there was one cutting board, one sharp knife (kept elsewhere) to be handled by an adult, serving plates, a mixing bowl, spoons, measuring cups and spoons, carrots, broccoli florets, cherry tomatoes, parsley leaves, yogurt, light sour cream, honey, cucumbers, and lettuce.

The recipes were: trees in a broccoli forest, rice, apple pie and a glass of milk, turkey and cheese sandwich, tuna and bean salad, and fruit smoothie.

Children at each table made sure their fresh fruits and vegetables were washed. The team leader was in charge of reading the recipe. Parent volunteers helped kids use plastic knives, turn on the stove, and adjust the large amount of ingredients because the original recipes were meant for two to four people. The adults and children multiplied the fractions in the recipes in order to have enough servings for the entire class. Throughout this process, the children were completely in charge. The kitchen staff came in to watch. It was amazing to see how seriously students took their tasks, and how enthusiastically they worked in teams, shared utensils, and shared common ingredients. For example, the sandwich makers waited for the protein group to hand them turkey and cheese slices; the teacher stepped back to admire this collaboration. At first, the students used the cutting board religiously to cut their veggies with the plastic knives, but soon some began to use only the tabletop to cut, until one student, Nur, reminded them, "Don't use the table, it's gonna scratch!" Mya defended their actions, "My vegetable slips out! I am trying, but I can't cut anything." "Cutting vegetables is hard, isn't it?" said Yan. "Not if we can use the real knife." "We are not allowed!" Shami sliced her bananas neatly and stacked them in layers on a plate. The teacher complemented her: "This looks nice." "My mom does that," Shami said. Amy also said, "Don't forget to keep all the seeds and vegetable covers in our soil pot!" Erin looked puzzled and corrected, "Not covers, they are called peels." The funniest part of the event involved the blender. On their first try, the students piled fruits and juice inside the blender and, without covering it with a lid, Mia turned it on. Whoosh! Everyone was instantly splashed with fruit smoothie, including me. Mia's face turned red, and her mom, who had volunteered, gushed out, "OH NO!" Everyone panicked and the table was a mess; Mia began crying. The teacher eventually stepped in to calm matters, while volunteers and students wiped away the spills. Soon everyone went back to their chores. After two-and-a-half hours of nonstop fun and exploration, they were all done. The principal and the office staff were invited to our food festival. There were compliments, happy remarks, and generally cheerful sentiments floating around. Parent volunteers and the teacher decided that they would write about the event in the class yearbook.

In order to keep the children focused on the topic, the teacher arranged cutout pictures of various kinds of foods all over the room. She had collected food labels and empty food containers, many of which were donated by parents. She asked students to help her to set up the grocery store according to the five food groups. Our tomato, carrot, and cilantro pot plants were displayed proudly near the grocery store, and students were able to use some cilantro during the cooking project. The teacher also noticed that children voluntarily continued the activity during recess and center time by playing with food items, reading labels, and pretending to go shopping.

Nutrition Bag

The nutrition bag contained photocopied food pyramid guidelines, lists of foods that make up the five food groups, tips for parents on how to incorporate the food groups into their daily diets, additional nutrition information for kids, and the "My Pyramid" worksheet. There were also photocopied recipes for the punch buggy pancakes, banana smoothie, vegetable pasta with fresh tomatoes, tuna and bean salad, and banana bread. The teacher included a letter requesting parents go on the Internet to look for the My Pyramid Blast Off Game, which they could play with their children. Finally, the bag had a list of some selected books available at the public library for kids to read at home, including *Blueberries for Sal* by Robert McCloskey, *Pancakes, Pancakes!* by Eric Carle, and *The Carrot Seed* by Ruth Krauss. The activities at home included: make butter, bread dough clay, crossword puzzles, MyPyramid.gov, Pyramid Go Fish instructions and laminated food cards, and packets of seeds and tips for growing indoor and outdoor vegetables.

After the cooking project, a few changes occurred in the class. Amy and Amnish, who usually ate chips and candy, decided to settle for granola bars and fruits (though Amnish did confess that he had a half of a fruit roll-up during snack time). The students began to read labels and ingredients wherever they found them with greater frequency.

Findings: Teacher 3

The pre-kindergarten teacher said, "It is becoming commonplace for many children to eat McDonald's, fried foods, and junk food on a normal, day-to-day basis. When asked about their favorite drink, the average answer is,

'We like 7 Up and Pepsi!' All children should become aware of the food pyramid, the different kinds of food, and how much they should consume on a daily basis in order for them to live more healthy and active lives."

At the end of the project, the teacher asked students what they'd learned. The two most popular answers were, "It is important to eat healthy so that we can be strong and grow more" and "If we don't eat healthy, we will not grow too much."

Thus, at the culmination of the project, the class had a better understanding of how eating healthy makes bones strong, makes skin more beautiful, and provides much-needed energy. The teacher also told her students about the importance of exercising and being active; one boy said, "Yeah, I do that when I go to the park." The teacher then asked, "How many of you have about a cup and a half of veggies every day?" "How many of you have about three to five pieces of fruit a day?" They all looked at the teacher in shock and said, "Not me." The teacher told the children that we should eat more servings of fruit.

Overall, the children also enjoyed the cooking project. They were very involved with making banana bread, and the teacher did not have to help them mix it. Indeed, one boy did it all by himself. Also, there were mini-lessons involved in this project; for example, one lesson involved learning the difference between a teaspoon, tablespoon, and one-quarter of a cup, which kids didn't know about until the teacher explained it to them.

To ensure that learning continues at home, the teacher gave the bag to three parents and asked the children if they enjoyed the nutrition bag. They said: "I liked the coloring book;" "I liked the recipes—mango smoothie, blueberry muffins, and fruit salad;" and "I liked the *Ten Apples* book by Dr. Seuss."

From the three surveys conducted of the parents, almost all the scores were 5s, which means that the parents strongly felt the instructions were simple, they enjoyed the activities, they would suggest the activities to other parents, they felt it taught them valuable information, and they felt the bag helped them bond with their children. All three especially liked the recipes section.

Findings: Teacher 4

The first-grade teacher gathered the children on the carpet and her first question was, "What did everyone eat for breakfast and snack today?"

All the children were eager to participate and volunteer their answers. They briefly discussed the types of food they usually eat for breakfast and snack. The teacher then asked them to go back to their seats and draw a picture of their usual breakfast and snack. When they were finished, everyone returned to the carpet in a circle to review and discuss each child's drawing. As they went through each drawing, the teacher wrote the name of the food on the board in two different groups. One group contained foods such as cereal, yogurt, bananas, grapes, and pancakes. The other group contained items such as cookies, cake, candy, chocolate, chips, and ice cream. Then the teacher asked the children to look at the board and compare the two groups (Group A consisted of healthy foods and Group B of unhealthy foods). Here are some examples of what they said:

Brian: "Group B is all snacks and Group A is not."

Mike: "Group A is good foods and Group B is bad foods."

Jim: "Group A are foods you should eat and Group B are foods you shouldn't eat."

Rayan: "Group A are healthy foods that are good for you and Group B is not."

The teacher then explained to the children that the key words of the day were "healthy" and "nutrition." The teacher then began a class discussion by asking children to name things we can do to help our bodies stay healthy. Some of the answers included exercising, brushing your teeth, taking baths, washing your hands, and eating healthy. Her next question was, "What kinds of food help keep us healthy?" Their responses mainly included different types of fruits and vegetables as well as milk. She then discussed how our bodies need over forty different nutrients for good health and no one food contains them all; thus, she said, we must eat a variety of foods each day to get the energy, protein, vitamins, minerals, and fiber we need to maintain healthy bodies. At this point, she introduced the food pyramid to the children and their interest in the topic heightened, as most of them had never seen it before. The class talked about each of the five food groups and discussed the variety of foods found within each group. The children further identified the three food groups they need to eat the most servings of every day.

The next step was to read a book to the class. The teacher read *What We Eat: A First Look at Food,* which introduces children to the different food groups and the origins of food, and gives them ideas for healthy meals. After reading, the teacher asked the children to draw the same thing they had earlier, but this time to draw a healthy snack and breakfast. When they completed their drawings, she broke the class into four groups to work on two different activities. The first two groups worked on making a healthy food collage; they were given food magazines and supermarket flyers and asked to cut out pictures of healthy foods. The last two groups were given paper and asked to fold the paper in half. They were told to draw "healthy" foods on one side and "not healthy" foods on the other. At the end of the small group activities, children gathered on the rug once more to review each other's work and discuss what they had learned about nutrition.

When reviewing what they had learned about eating healthy, here are some examples of some of the children's reactions:

Teacher: "What did we learn about nutrition today?"

Rayan: "You shouldn't eat too many cookies, chips, and ice cream. You should only eat them once in a while."

Teacher: "Why not?"

Rayan: "Because it is not healthy for you."

Mike: "Yeah, it's junk."

Jim: "And they all have a lot of sugar."

Teacher: "What does sugar do to you?"

Matt: "It makes you crazy."

Ali: "It makes your teeth rotten and fall out."

Brian: "It gives you cavities."

Teacher: "What else did you learn today?"

Jeff: "We should eat a lot of fruits, vegetables, and grains."

Tim: "And meats, chicken, beans, and milk."

Matt: "We should only eat ice cream, cookies, cake, and candy sometimes."

Erin: "Cheerios and Kix are good for you because they don't have sugar. Some cereals are bad for you."

To reinforce the importance of nutrition and healthy eating, the teacher taught the class three songs. They learned a song about fruits, vegetables, and grains. Before the lesson she wrote the songs on large chart paper and hung them on the board. She read the songs to the class and then asked them to read them with her. Once they were able to read the songs by themselves, they sang the songs on their own. The children enjoyed singing because the songs were sung to tunes that were familiar to them. For example, "The Vegetable Song" was sung to the tune of "Twinkle, Twinkle, Little Star."

Throughout the project, the children needed very little help or assistance. It was easy for them to draw what they normally eat for breakfast and lunch because they were referencing their own experiences. They also enjoyed sharing with the class because they felt confident in their presentation of this information. When the teacher composed the two lists of healthy and not healthy foods, the children were immediately able to distinguish between the two without any prompting. When discussing nutrition as a class, the children were willing to learn new facts and did not need to be motivated to participate. While working in small groups, they worked very cooperatively with each other and did not ask for any help. If a child had a question or needed help with something, he or she would ask a fellow classmate in his or her group.

The teacher was able to send the nutrition bag home to two parents for two days each. Both parents returned the bag with positive feedback and said they enjoyed participating in the activities with their children. They agreed the nutrition bag was very helpful in teaching their children basic concepts of nutrition and vegetables, and noted that their children were excited about participating in most of the activities in the bag. The two parents also agreed that their children's awareness of the uses, appearance, and spelling of vegetables had somewhat increased, as well as their recognition of and appreciation for nutritious foods, and that their kids had a better understanding of the health contribution of different foods because of the nutrition bag. The first parent commented that the multicultural recipes were the most helpful activity in the bag. Her child is a mix of Italian and Irish, so they made the recipes from Italy and Ireland together. The parent expressed great joy in this activity and said it was extremely helpful in teaching her child how different cultures can prepare the same foods in completely different ways. She also said there was nothing in the nutrition bag that wasn't helpful and that she wouldn't make any changes to it. The second parent found the memory card game to be the most beneficial for her child. She said that it was a fun and easy way for her child to learn the different types of vegetables. She explained how her child becomes easily distracted in his work if he is not interested in it, and said that he was completely interested in the game and wanted to keep playing. She also commented on how the game was exactly right for his level and he was excited about playing the game in three different ways. Whenever he tried to play it in a new way, he was motivated to keep going because each way presented a new challenge, enough to keep him interested. From the parents' perspective, the nutrition bag had an overall positive effect on both the children and their parents. In general, the nutrition bag was a huge success as it provided opportunities for children to gain a better understanding of the importance of nutrition, engage in fun yet meaningful learning activities, and gave the parents a chance to become involved in their child's learning experience.

The teacher also had a brief discussion with the two children who took the nutrition bag home. They both liked the contents in the bag and explained how the activities were fun. When the teacher spoke with the first child, she asked her what her favorite part of the bag was; the child said, "I got to cook with my mom. We made food from Italy and Ireland and it was really good." She also talked about how she liked reading the vegetable jokes with her mom. The second child explained his favorite part of the bag: "I liked the memory game, the crosswords, and the coloring pictures." He explained how he also liked all the games and activities, fun facts, and jokes that were in the binder. He talked about how he and his mom sat together at nighttime and did a lot of the different activities in the binder. Although both children liked different parts of the nutrition bag, they both agreed the contents were fun, they learned new things, and they had a good time working with their parents.

Discussion

The main objective of this project was to help children understand health and increase their capacity to select nutritious food, and thus, their ability to lead healthy lives.

Many of the teachers who participated felt that this was an important project for children to engage in. Most teachers felt personal gratification that their students were able to identify and select healthy foods at the culmination of the project. It was an eye-opening learning experience for the children, as well as for the teachers.

Children learned and had fun throughout the project. They could find the link between what they were learning in the classroom and their personal lives. The teachers made better connections with children and with their parents. Parents liked the connection to the school and felt that their children were learning and enjoying themselves in class. Children were also exposed to language arts, math, science, social studies, and music skills through this topic. Further, in some cases, the regular classroom teacher, and in others, the school administration, appreciated and benefited from this unit. Therefore, if teachers and parents want to inspire the children to learn about health and choosing healthy food from an early age, it is clear that activities that engage students in actively learning about food have a great impact on their learning.

SUMMARY

- Numerous studies have proved the link between nutrition and academic performance as measured by test scores, attendance rates, tardiness, and discipline.
- Children are in school for a substantial part of the day, and teachers play a critical role in helping students learn healthy eating habits.
- The maintenance of a healthy weight starting in childhood is a strong factor in avoiding many of the additional health risks that have been associated with obesity.
- Young children need to learn about nutrition, health, and personal hygiene.
- If children are involved in the process of making nutritional food for themselves, then they will be able to select the right kind of food and take care of their health.

Thinking Questions

1. List the foods that children need for a balanced diet.
2. How would you help children to develop a healthy habit of selecting nutritional foods?
3. What are the food safety protocols a child needs to know at home, in school, and in the community?

REFERENCES

Cosgrove, M. S. (1991). Cooking in the classroom: The doorway to nutrition. *Young Children, 46*(3), 43–46.

ERIC Digest. ED369580 1994-06-00 Nutrition Programs for Children. http://files.eric.ed.gov/fulltext/ED369580.pdf.

Fuhr, J. E., & Barclay, K. H. (1998). The importance of appropriate nutrition and nutrition education. *Young Children, 53*(1), 74–80.

Jacobson, L. (2004). Preschoolers' choice: Tofu or potato chips? *Education Week, 23*(32).

Kendrick, A. S., Kaufmann, R., & Messenger, K. P. (Eds.) (1995). *Healthy young children: A manual for programs.* Washington, DC: National Association for the Education of Young Children.

McDonald, W. F., Brun, J. K., & Esserman, J. (1981). In-home interviews measure positive effects of a school nutrition program. *Journal of Nutrition Education, 13*(4), 140–44.

Montessori (1965). Excerpt from Early Childhood Education Today, by G.S. Morrison, 2009 edition, p. 140–143.

Morrison, G. S. (1998). *Early Childhood Education Today* (7th ed.). Englewood Cliffs, NJ: Prentice-Hall.

Neergaard, L. (2006, December 29). Study: Many kids too fat by preschool. *San Francisco Chronicle*. Retrieved from http://sfgate.com/cgibin/article.cgi?file=/n/a/2006/12/28/national/w142359S40.DTL.

New York City Department of Education Wellness Policies on Physical Activity and Nutrition June 2010. Retrieved from http://schools.nyc.gov/NR/rdonlyres/2B99376C-5BA2-4D97-9F85-1C5DA395EFF4/0/NYCDOEWellnessPolicy_June2010.pdf.

Seefeldt, C., & Galper, A. (2002). *Active experiences for active children - science.* Upper Saddle River, NJ: Pearson Education.

Sutherland, R., Gill, T., & Binns, C. (2004). Do parents, teachers and health professionals support school-based obesity prevention? *Nutrition & Dietetics, 61*(3), 137–144.

Swadener, S. S. (1995). Nutrition education for preschool children. *Journal of Nutrition Education, 27*(6), 291–97.

Wardle, J., Herrera, M. L., Cooke, L., Gibson, E. L. (2003). Modifying children's food preferences: the effects of exposure and reward on acceptance of an unfamiliar vegetable. *European Journal of Clinical Nutrition, 57*(2) 341–8.

BOOK LISTS

Brown, W. M. (1996). *Big Red Barn.* HarperCollins Children's Books.
Brown, M. (1947). *Stone Soup.* Simon & Schuster.
Carle, E. (1992). *Pancakes, Pancakes!* Scholastic.
Carle, E. (1993). *Today Is Monday.* Scholastic.

Cooper, H. (1998). *Pumpkin Soup*.
Dooley, N. (1992). *Everybody Cooks Rice*. Learner Publishing Group.
Dr. Seuss (1960). *Just For Kids*. (2004). NY: L&D Publications.
Dr. Seuss. (1961). *Ten Apples Up On Top!* Random House.
Krauss, R. (1993). *The Carrot Seed*. HarperCollins Children's Books.
McCloskey, R. (1976). *Blueberries for Sal*. Penguin Young Readers Group.
Robson, R. (1997). *What's for lunch? Bananas*. Children's Press.

WEBSITES

www.bread.com/grains.php
www.dole5aday.com
www.enchantedlearning.com/foods ("Going Shopping" reproducible book)
www.healthrecipes.com
www.gotmilk.com
www.kidshealth.org
http://library.thinkquest.org/07aug/00263/08_Food_Pyramids.html
www.nutritionexplorations.org
nycenet.edu/default.aspx (New York City Department of Education)
www.parentinghumor.com/activitycenter/songrhymes.htm ("Making Bread" song)
www.pbskids.org
www.thegardenhelper.com
www.wheatmania.com
www.tinytummies.com

Chapter Seven

Helping Children to Be Successful in Life

Every child is blessed with certain unique qualities. It is the responsibility of adults to nurture these qualities in children and work with them to resolve topics, skills, or subjects they find challenging. After all, early childhood is an important period, where the essence of a person's character is formed; thus, what happens in this period determines an individual's capacity to become a leader in the future.

Early childhood is also a critical period in the development of communicative competence. Communication, expression, and reasoning are strengthened when children engage in discussion. Teachers play an important role in encouraging this development by actively listening and providing positive feedback to children, such as "that's true," or "that's interesting," and more. Further, dinner table discussions with family members also help children with key communication skills.

Through group discussions, leadership games, team-building exercises, informative lectures, and simulation games, children identify their own particular leadership strengths, create their personal goals, and develop a commitment to community service.

THE FAMILY AND PARENT'S ROLE

Families have diverse and distinct characteristics that make each family a unique entity. It is the parents who hold the child's hand in the outer world. Parents protect children for as long as they need it, and are there for them through good and bad. They provide guidance, direction, help, and assistance as needed.

Ultimately, parents have to be responsible for their children's actions. They are the child's first teacher. Parents have to teach them wisely about being polite, and respecting others and themselves. Parents must also take time out of their busy weeks to have fun with children. Parents should take their children on trips. A family trip offers children great experiences and offers wonderful learning opportunities. Before a trip, parents should ask children about what they hope to find, help them research information on the destination, work with them to develop an itinerary for the trip, and encourage them to record their reflections and thoughts in journals while traveling. Parents can also encourage their children to read environmental print.

Parents should teach children experiences from their lives. Storytelling is one very effective technique, and oftentimes, stories about parents growing up create bonds between parents and children.

It is important to teach children to obey rules around the house to prepare them for the future. When children need moral support, parents build their confidence up and motivate them to achieve more. It is also important to let the children know that as long as they've tried their very best, they will never lose the respect and love of their parents.

Taking children to respective religious schools and exposing them to religious beliefs helps them to get a good solid base for growing up. Parents should teach children about nature and how to care for and respect it. Parents should also teach children about morals and ethics. It is important to teach children how to be kind and compassionate toward others. Giving children a happy childhood is the main role of a parent.

THE TEACHER'S ROLE

A teacher's role in a child's life is immense. Teachers should provide rich experiences to all of their students; establishing learning goals for individual children is an important part of this. Teachers need to plan their lessons thinking of each child. It is important to remember that children will have larger vocabularies if they are exposed to words through conversations and shared reading activities. Children learn sight words when they dictate their stories and adults transcribe them.

Young children should enjoy learning new things and not be pressured into outdoing each other or made to feel inferior. Such experiences in early childhood have an impact on their capacity to develop later. According to Katz (1988), knowledge, skills, disposition, and feelings are the four categories of learning. Generally, knowledge and skills are what parents and schools worry about most. However, disposition is very different. Disposition could be thought of as habits of the mind. For example, curiosity is a disposition. Dispositions are not learned through instruction.

We want children to be curious, cooperative, friendly, helpful, and hardworking. However, children's dispositions can be affected by the way we set up tasks for them. For example, if we create categories of "best" and "worst" in the classroom, we foster a spirit of competition and not collaboration among children. Further, children become very anxious to show their best and their anxiety may negatively impact their performance. Feelings are subjective emotional states. Teachers and parents need to make sure that children maintain an inclination toward curiosity and an interest in learning, because inquiry-based learning leads the learner to understand something on their own. Through projects and interesting group-based activities, children have fun and learn at the same time.

Preschools and nursery schools should provide opportunities for social interaction. Let children explore. Stimulating activities increase children's attention and interest. It is better to provide learning goals than performance goals. Learning goals allow children to achieve something. If children relate to a task or topic in school, they have a better chance of becoming interested in learning and are therefore less likely to feel incompetent. They will further develop a community feeling.

Developing social competence builds self-esteem. For example, children who are friendly become more attractive to and popular among their peers. Gaining acceptance from friends becomes very important for children as they grow up. Thus, these early years are especially crucial for social competence later in life.

During free playtime, teachers should take the opportunity to observe how children are playing with their peers, and particularly how they are building friendships. This is especially important if children are shy and introverted; in early childhood, teachers are best positioned to help these children make friends. Teachers can also make play more effective by using open-ended materials, such as sand, water, Legos, and blocks. Children can use these materials for play together and also separately. Playing outside not only helps children's gross motor development, but also encourages overall health because it provides opportunities for children to breathe fresh air and get oxygen.

Becoming interested in a topic helps children to get deeply involved in that topic. Using the project-based approach is often very effective among children. Building on preexisting knowledge, children's curiosity should be nurtured. Let children wonder and ask questions. Help children find answers using technology, interviewing experts, observing, and experimenting to gather knowledge. Students should record their ideas and knowledge in their journal by writing, drawing, and taking pictures. Therefore, a project-based approach is an effective way to teach children a topic in depth.

If children are praised for achieving a specific goal or task, they will want to do better in the future. Teachers should give positive feedback that is informative. Simply stating "good job" will not serve to increase productivity. Even when children feel feedback is not necessary for the completion of a project, it inevitably increases their interest in it. Positive feedback is important; finding the right moment to give it is sometimes difficult for teachers to figure out, but necessary.

It is important to remember that routines are created to help children, but should not be followed at their expense. This means that children should not be rushed to go to gym, music, and so on, because it is time. A hurried child is more likely to have issues focusing on tasks later in life. Rather, teachers and parents should set tentative schedules so that children sense the general sequence with which they should complete activities.

THE COMMUNITY'S ROLE

The community has a great role to play in the lives of the children. Community members should strive to create learning opportunities for children. Such opportunities occur when children meet experts in various fields, many of whom can come from the community itself. For example, one set of "experts" could be a child's parents, who often have skills and knowledge in different areas. Groups within the community should gather these kinds of resources for children. If the community has a difficult time gathering experts from among its own members, parents should reach out to other communities, or look into their own community resources.

Once children are exposed to a program, then parents can be sought after as resources for field trips. For example, if a parent works as a real estate agent, then the parent can show different kinds of houses to children. A parent who is an architect can show blueprints for houses, and similarly, a construction worker can lead the children on site visits. Children should reflect on all of these kinds of experiences in personal journals to maximize and memorialize what they've learned.

Community members can also create shows for children and encourage them to engage in discussion after shows. Children could be invited for a magic show and then be shown the magic behind the scenes. After a puppet show, there could be a workshop about how to create puppets and then an opportunity for the children to make up a show. Then as part of a follow-up to the show, the children who took an active part in the workshop the previous time could be involved in the next production.

During the summer months or after-school hours, an art class or a sculpture class could be offered to the children. Music for everyone and dance class could be other areas. Various sports activities could attract the children, as well.

During our children's lives, technology will advance and impact them. They have to communicate as leaders. Technology is advancing by leaps and bounds, and children need to have access to such technology to keep pace. Libraries often provide a source of free access to current technology. Communities also play an important role in acclimating children to technology, which is advancing rapidly and will impact them in the future.

A community should provide programs guiding children into leadership roles. Such programs should accomplish the following:

- Identify methods for becoming a leader.
- Demonstrate how leadership evolves.
- Demonstrate ways to improve communication skills.
- Show children how different parts of communities work effectively together.
- Help children identify career possibilities.
- Build relationships and network with other community leaders.

- Practice team building with children and help them maintain contact with others.
- Show children how they can make a difference in the lives of others and make the world a better place.

All of us are responsible for helping our children become well-rounded individuals. It is important to stimulate them so they are better thinkers, more capable of taking challenges while analyzing and assessing risks. If we care for our children, they will learn to care for others. Positive developmental growth also means they will be more independent, more self-disciplined, and have greater self-esteem. These aspects of character development, which occur in early childhood, are key determinants of success in the future.

Ultimately, children will become successful with the help of the community. It is true that parents are the first teachers of their children. If parents are aware of all the resources in the environment and strategies that are needed to enrich their children's lives, then they have the capacity to fully enrich their children's lives and provide the groundwork for academic and social success. Parents need to be aware of the health and nutrition needs of their children. They also should be aware of what strategies the teachers are taking in the school; the type of enriched curriculum that their children are involved in; how their children are learning through play; and how their children are delving deep in the project-based approach. All adults involved in the children's lives should be observing the children and keeping regular logs of their achievements and also address their challenges. This is true of all children: with or without disabilities, gifted and/or talented, multilingual with different ethnic backgrounds, and English language learners. All adults involved with children have a moral obligation to meet the needs of all children because children are so vulnerable yet too valuable, and they are going to be our future leaders. Truly it takes a village to raise a child to ensure success.

SUMMARY

- Early childhood is a critical period in the development of an individual's communicative competence.

- Parents are responsible for their children's actions. Teach children to obey rules around the house to prepare them for the future, and convey moral and ethical standards.
- Teachers should provide rich experiences to all of their students.
- Communities could create programs with shows, which include discussions with parents and children.

Thinking Questions

1. What are the measures of success?
2. Develop long-term strategies that would help children achieve their goals.
3. What are the different ways to make children successful?

REFERENCES

Elkind, K. (1988) *The hurried child: Growing up too fast too soon* (3rd ed.). New York: Perseus Books Group.

Katz, L G. (1988). What should young children be doing? *American Educator: The Professional Journal of the American Federation of Teachers, 12*(2), 28–33, 44–45.

Appendix A

EXAMPLE 1 OF RUNNING RECORD:
DANNY IN DRAMATIC PLAY

Center/Age Level: P.S. 111/Pre–K
Date: 10/30
Observer: Ms. Mangrove

Time: 9:38–10:10 a.m.
Child: Danny/3;11
Teacher: Ms. Anders
Assistant: Ms. Kaplocs

Observation	Comments
Danny and three other children (two girls and one other boy) are assigned to the dramatic play area by Ms. Anders. Danny does not get up immediately until the teacher calls him again to the center.	9:38 a.m. Does not seem enthusiastic about going to the center. He has to be called twice. Is he not willing to listen, or might he have a hearing problem?
He walks slowly to the dramatic play area and wanders around the kitchen area rolling his head. He makes a swishing noise as he walks toward the area. The other children begin to play cooking together. Danny chooses not to be a part of the group. He wanders and plays with the cash register.	While the other children seem to have a plan in mind when entering the center, Danny seems unfamiliar with the items in the center.
He pushes the buttons on the register and discovers the play money in the register. He takes out the play coins and puts them on a plate that is found next to the register. He mumbles something to himself as he takes out the coins one by one.	9:41 a.m. Is he counting to himself? He needs to pay more attention.

Observation	Comments
One little girl approaches Danny and asks him if he wants to cook. She says, "We're playing cooking, do you want to cook?" Danny looks at the girl but does not reply. Instead he walks away from her and walks toward the play sink and pretends to wash his hands.	Why doesn't he like to participate with the group? Is he shy or intimidated by his language barrier?
He takes a look at the foods that are laid out on the table that were prepared by the other children and grabs one of the pizza slices. A boy says, "Stop, that's our pizza. I made it." Danny looks up surprised, puts back the pizza, and walks away. He goes toward the area where the musical instrument basket is and pulls on the xylophone. He stretches for the basket and looks for help to get the instrument. He sees me and uses his hand to gesture, by pointing to the basket while looking to me to help him get the basket down. Yet he doesn't say a word.	9:43 a.m. Seems interested in what the other children cooked, but inappropriately grabs the work of others. When the other child tells him to stop, was he discouraged to join the group? Although he doesn't speak much, he uses his body language to ask for help.
He takes a drumstick from the basket and hits the xylophone. Then he takes another stick from the basket and hits the xylophone with the other stick. He notices a slightly different sound and goes back to using the first stick.	9:44 a.m. Able to notice sound differentiations.
Danny is called to the art table for the daily art project.	9:45–9:56 a.m.
Danny comes back to the kitchen area and plays with the musical instruments again. The other children walk around him as they go about their playing. Some have moved on to playing with the strollers and dolls while others are playing with the telephone and cash register. Danny is in front of the kitchen area, and the children move about without saying much to him or seeming to be aware of his existence. When he is in the way, however, the children simply squeeze by him.	9:56 a.m. Children seem to ignore him. Doesn't seem to mind not interacting with the other children.
Danny continues to play alone with the food and the plates in the kitchen area. He sets up two places on the table and mixes the food items together in a pot and serves them onto the two plates.	9:58 a.m. Able to role play on his own and understands representation; however, engages in parallel play more often than group play.

Observation	Comments
He licks his lips as he is serving the food. Then he makes another unidentifiable sound.	
Danny continues to play alone with the food and the plates in the kitchen area. He sets up two places on the table and mixes the food items together in a pot and serves them onto the two plates. He licks his lips as he is serving the food. Then he makes another unidentifiable sound.	10:08 a.m. Able to be a helpful team player when it is clean-up time.

Interpretation

Danny seems to have trouble engaging in group play and communication with others. The other children seem to also leave him out of their activity since he does not seem to be at the same play level as the others. It may be helpful for the teacher to guide the other children to include Danny in their group activity so that he feels comfortable with others. The teacher also needs to help Danny learn to interact and develop confidence in playing with others. He needs to strengthen his social skills. A play date with his classmates could be a good idea.

EXAMPLE 2 OF RUNNING RECORD: RACHEL

School: P.S. 300　　　　　　　　　　Time: 9:10 a.m.
Date: 9/29/2009　　　　　　　　　　Child/Age: Rachael/3
Observer: Maria

Observation	Comments
The child comes to the rug for circle time. She has her feet spread out in front of her. Rather than having her eyes facing the teacher, her eyes are looking upward. The child is not saying anything during circle time. She does not have any comments as the teacher does the read aloud.	9:10 a.m. Seems to not be following the patterns of the other children, seems to be in her own world. 9:12 a.m. Maybe the girl is shy, she might be scared to have the wrong answer, she may not be fully listening to the story.

Observation	Comments
The child fidgets with her fingers on the rug. She is moving her fingers in a twirling motion.	9:13 a.m. This may be too long for the child to sit, seems that the child has excess energy to release, maybe she gets distracted easily.
The child is not singing along with the class as the other children sing a song about the season of fall. She is not participating in any of the dance movements.	9:15 a.m. Again, I think she may be a very shy, conservative girl, maybe at home she is not used to being surrounded by singing and dancing.

Interpretation

The child has trouble cooperating during circle time. She has a very hard time focusing when she is not the one speaking. She seems to be eager to speak and when she cannot she gazes off into her own world. I believe that the teacher should elicit more feedback from her during circle time to make sure she is paying attention.

EXAMPLE 1 OF ANECDOTAL RECORD

Observation

9/29/06 Aidan (4;3). While playing at his table with connecting block pieces during free playtime, Aidan connected several of these pieces together vertically. He added several pieces more until his creation toppled to the table. Aidan took the remaining pieces apart and started building again, but this time he built his creation horizontally so it laid flat on the table. He turned to the teacher and said, "When I put it taller it breaks" (cognitive-reasoning).

Interpretation

Aidan had tried to build what looked like a ladder with the connecting building blocks. He was building it vertically and was trying to make it taller by adding more block pieces. It kept falling onto the table. After several tries, Aidan probably thought that it would not break and fall if he laid it flat on the table while connecting the blocks. He may have also noticed that by laying his creation flat on the table, he was able to add more block pieces to make it longer. This reasoning could have occurred to him because on the other side of the table several of his classmates were taking the same type of blocks and building railroad tracks with them. Their tracks were getting longer without breaking as more pieces were added. Aidan may have noticed this and wanted to experiment with his creation by laying it flat on the table just like their tracks. His use of "taller" may actually mean that when his creation is standing up, it breaks.

EXAMPLE 2 OF ANECDOTAL RECORD

Observation

10/2/06 Aidan (4;3). After snack time Aidan stood next to the lunchbox shelf as his classmates were putting away their lunchboxes. He left a space next to his lunchbox and placed his arm in this space. As his classmates put their lunchboxes on the shelf he told them, "I'm saving this for Emily's" (psychosocial-friendship).

Interpretation

Aidan seems to have formed a very strong bond with Emily. Last week the children arrived at school Monday to discover that their seating arrangements had been changed. Emily was no longer at Aidan's table. She had sat across from him since the first day of school and they must have formed a special friendship. Since the day their seats were changed, Aidan has made sure to place his lunchbox next to hers on the shelf. When they sat at the same table he did not show this behavior. He even has gone so far as to switch his other classmates' lunchboxes if they are next to hers if he arrives at school after them. However, today's incident was the first time Aidan verbally expressed to his classmates that he wants the space next to his lunchbox reserved only for Emily's lunchbox. The lunchbox arrangement seems to be very important to Aidan, and perhaps this is his way of keeping a close psychological bond with Emily now that they are seated away from each other.

EXAMPLE 3 OF ANECDOTAL RECORD

Observation

While waiting in line for dismissal lineup in the classroom, Danny arbitrarily hits another child who was lining up behind him. When the teacher spoke with him about hitting, he did not seem to show any remorse for hitting. He stared blankly at the teacher when she explained to him that he shouldn't hit, and when he was asked to say sorry, he said it without seeming to understand why.

Interpretation

Danny hits a child in the face out of the blue. He seems to not be able to keep his hands to himself. He has a hard time standing still and waiting in line. Maybe the teacher can try to not let him get ready too early. He's dressed the earliest and may be antsy and tired of waiting for all the children to get dressed.

EXAMPLE OF ABC NARRATIVE

Center: Applebees Childcare Inc.   Time: 8:30 a.m.–12 p.m.
Date: 10/22, 10/23   Child/age: Taylor/2.6
Observer: Melissa   Teacher: Janice
Target Behavior: Not following directions

Date: 10/22	Antecedent	Behavior	Consequence
8:30 a. m.	Eating breakfast with other toddlers.	Ate her cereal and when she was done would not sit in her seat and wait for the other children to finish. She kept sitting on the floor whining.	Teacher tells Taylor to sit in her seat and wait for everyone else. Redirects her by telling her she will get a sticker on her chart if she stays seated.

Date: 10/22	Antecedent	Behavior	Consequence
10:30 a.m.	Story time (circle time) where everyone sits together on the carpet.	Taylor sits for about five minutes and seems interested, and then suddenly starts drifting away and begins to play alone with other toys.	Teachers say to Taylor to please get back on the carpet and pay attention to the story with friends. Teacher tells her that she will stop reading the story unless she gets back on the carpet.
Date: 10/23			
9:30 a.m.	During free play, Taylor is playing with many connector links.	Another child comes by to play with her with links. Taylor says, "NO," and would not share with anyone else. She began throwing a fit and screaming. Teacher goes to her and says to please share with the other children. Taylor continues to ignore the teacher and does not share.	Teacher takes all links away from Taylor and says that she can only play with the links if she shares.
12 p.m.	TV time before lunch. Everyone is sitting on the carpet to watch a movie and no free play is allowed at this time.	Taylor leaves the carpet after five minutes of watching the movie and begins to take toys to play with. Teacher says she must put down the toys and sit with her friends to enjoy the movie. Taylor screams out, "NO," and does not stop playing.	Teacher takes the toys away, places her on the carpet and explains to her that it is movie time and we must sit with our friends. She lies down and begins to whine.

Appendix A

EXAMPLE OF CHECKLIST

Center/Age: (P.S. 1000/3- to 4-year-olds)   Child/Age: Rachel/3
Date: 10/13/2009   Teacher: Ms. Armstead
Observer: Maria

Topic: Fine Motor Skills for preschool children

☐ 1) Is able to firmly grasp a pencil and crayon when writing or drawing.

☐ 2) Is able to hold a paintbrush.

☐ 3) Is able to cut using scissors using the correct grip

☐ 4) Is able to manipulate play dough (rolling into small balls, long rolls, etc.)

☐ 5) Is able to tear paper into fine strips (using them for a collage, crumbling paper, etc.)

☐ 6) Is able to finger paint and manipulate other liquids with hands.

☐ 7) Is able to paste objects.

☐ 8) Is able to copy simple shapes.

☐ 9) Is able to zip a zipper.

☐ 10) Is able to isolate finger movements (ex. Count one at a time.)

Figure A1.   Fine Motor Skills for preschool children

Comments

Sources

http://www.maricopa.edu?dept/d46/psy/dev/Spring01/Preschool/skills.html
http://www.sensory-processing-disorder.com/fine-motor-skills-activities-for-
   children.html
http://www.bellaonline.com/articles/art27052.asp
http://www.getreadyforschool.com/index.html

Appendix B

EXAMPLE 1 OF RATING SCALE

Center/Age Level: P.S. 1200/Pre–K (4- to 5-year-olds)
Date/Time: October 10, 2013/8:30–10:30 a.m.
Observer: Maria

		Danny	Phyllis	Victoria	Ariel	Sammy
1.	Maintains eye contact when speaking.		√		√	√
2.	Listens to others while others speak.		√	√		√
3.	Shares toys with other children.		√			√
4.	Greets teachers and other children voluntarily.		√			√
5.	Sits alongside other children.		√	√		√
6.	Willingly converses with other children.		√			√
7.	Initiates conversation with another child.		√			√
8.	Partners up with another child easily.		√			√
9.	Joins play group voluntarily.		√			√
10.	Plays in groups of more than two.		√			√
11.	Willingness to share info about self with others.		√		√	√

		Danny	Phyllis	Victoria	Ariel	Sammy
12.	Approaches others without hesitation.		√			√
13.	Likes to play alone.	√			√	
14.	Shies away when other children approach.	√			√	

EXAMPLE 2 OF RATING SCALE

Center/Age Level: P.S. 3000/Pre–K (4- to 5-year-olds)
Date/Time: October 16, 2006/8:30–10:30 a.m.
Observer: Vladimir
Scale: 1=with ease   2=able to but slowly   3=requires help   4=unable to

		Danny	Phyllis	Victoria	Ariel	Sammy
1.	Runs with controlled starts and stops.	1	1	1	1	1
2.	Gallops with one leg.	2	3	3	2	2
3.	Can hop 7 to 9 times on one foot.	1	2	2	1	1
4.	Climbs up ladder.	1	1	1	1	1
5.	Climbs up stairs with alternating feet.	1	1	2	2	1
6.	Descends stairs with alternating feet.	2	2	2	2	2
7.	Skips with one foot.	1	1	1	1	1
8.	Catches a large ball.	4	3	2	3	1
9.	Throws a large ball.	2	2	2	1	1
10.	Throws a small ball.	1	1	2	1	1
11.	Catches a small ball.	4	4	4	3	2
12.	Begins a jump with a crouch.	2	2	3	2	1
13.	Hangs independently from overhead bar.	3	3	3	3	2
14.	Walks on a balance beam with alternating feet.	2	1	2	1	1
15.	Kicks a ball with foot.	1	1	2	3	1
16.	Twists with a hula hoop.	4	4	4	3	4

About the Author

Smita Guha is an Associate Professor in Early Childhood Education at St. John's University, New York. She has been a university faculty member for fifteen years and has over ten years of experience working with young children.